C000186030

MEMORIES OF
STOKE
ON TRENT

TRUE NORTH BOOKS

BRITANNIA WORKS GARDEN STREET NORTH
HALIFAX
WEST YORKSHIRE
HX3 6AE
TEL 01422 344344

THE PUBLISHERS WOULD LIKE TO THANK THE
FOLLOWING COMPANIES FOR SUPPORTING THE
PRODUCTION OF THIS BOOK

MAIN SPONSOR

FWB PRODUCTS LIMITED

ACME MARLS LIMITED

AYNSLEY CHINA LIMITED

JAMES T BLAKEMAN & COMPANY LIMITED

CAPPER RATAUD LIMITED

CHAMBERS ESTATES LIMITED

CITY OF STOKE-ON-TRENT SIXTH FORM COLLEGE

THE DUDSON GROUP

EW GOOD & COMPANY (LONGTON) LIMITED

GEO S HALL LIMITED

EG JAMES LIMITED

S KEELING & COMPANY LIMITED

KEELING & WALKER LIMITED

LYCETTS (BURSLEM) LIMITED

PORTMEIRION POTTERIES LIMITED

POTTERIES SHOPPING CENTRE

JESSE SHIRLEY & SON LIMITED

ARTHUR ROBERTS & SONS LIMITED

ROYAL DOULTON

ROYAL WINTON CHINA

SELECTUS LIMITED

SPODE

TAYLOR TUNNICLIFF LIMITED

WALKERS' NONSUCH LIMITED

First published in Great Britain by True North Books Limited, England HX3 6AE

© Copyright: True North Books Limited, 1998
This edition reprinted 2002

ISBN 1 900 463 47 4

Introduction

Welcome to *Memories of Stoke on Trent*, a look back on some of the places, events and people in the city which have shaped the lives of local people over a period of around half a century. The following pages are brought to life by a selection of images from the not-too-distant past, chosen according to their ability to rekindle fond memories of days gone by and show how people used to shop, work and play in the area where they grew up. Modern image reproduction techniques have enabled us to present these pictures in a way rarely seen before, and the lively design and informative text has attempted to set the book apart from some of the other works available.

The chosen period is one which generally contains events within the memory of a large number of people in Stoke on Trent - this is not a book about crinolines or bowler-hats! Neither is *Memories of Stoke on Trent* a work of local history in the normal sense of the term. It has far more to do with entertainment than serious study, but we hope you will agree it is none the worse for that. It is hoped that the following pages will prompt readers' own memories of Stoke on Trent from days gone by - and we are always delighted to hear from people who can add to the information contained in the captions so that we can enhance future editions of the book.

Many local companies and organisations have allowed us to study their archives and include their history - and fascinating reading it makes too. The present-day guardians of the firms concerned are proud of their products, the achievements of their people and the hard work of their forefathers whose efforts created these long established organisations in the first place. We are pleased to play our part by making it possible for them to share their history with a wider audience.

When we began compiling *Memories of Stoke on Trent* several months ago we anticipated that the task would be a pleasurable one, but our expectations were greatly surpassed. There is a growing appetite for all things 'nostalgic' and we are pleased to have played a small part in swelling the number of images and associated information available to the growing number of enthusiasts.

There is much talk in modern times about the regeneration of the local economy, the influx of new industries and the challenge of attracting new enterprise from other regions to Stoke on Trent. And quite right too. We could, however, make the mistake of thinking that the changes are all happening *now*, but the reality is that there have always been major developments going on in the city.

Change is relentless and the photographs on the pages in the book serve to remind us of some of them.

Memories of Stoke on Trent has been a pleasure to compile. We sincerely hope you enjoy reading it.

Happy memories!

TEXT	PEGGY BURNS
COVER DESIGN/PHOTOGRAPH COMPILATION	MARK SMITH
DESIGNERS	MANDY WALKER, NICKY BRIGHTON AND CHRISTINE GALE
BUSINESS DEVELOPMENT EDITOR	GARETH MARTIN

CONTENTS

Street life

The Warrillow Collection

Where did they all go to? Police officers on point duty, that is. There was a time when every major junction in every major town had its traffic 'bobby'; remember those black and white zebra-striped boxes they used to use? The boxes made them highly visible and gave them the elevation and air of authority they needed. Point duty must have demanded a high concentration of manpower, however, and it was no doubt argued that instead of directing the town's traffic the police force would be better employed in concentrating their efforts on the fight against crime.

So a few at a time they departed, leaving the motorist with a legacy of traffic lights to contend with at each junction. Traffic lights, while no doubt keeping the traffic flowing smoothly through the town centre (in theory at least), somehow lack the personal touch provided by the good old British bobby.

This policeman awaiting an opportunity to allow pedestrians to cross Piccadilly in Hanley was on duty sometime in the late 1930s. Once a Milk Bar, Swinnerton's Café along the road to the right became a well known place to obtain a tasty meal.

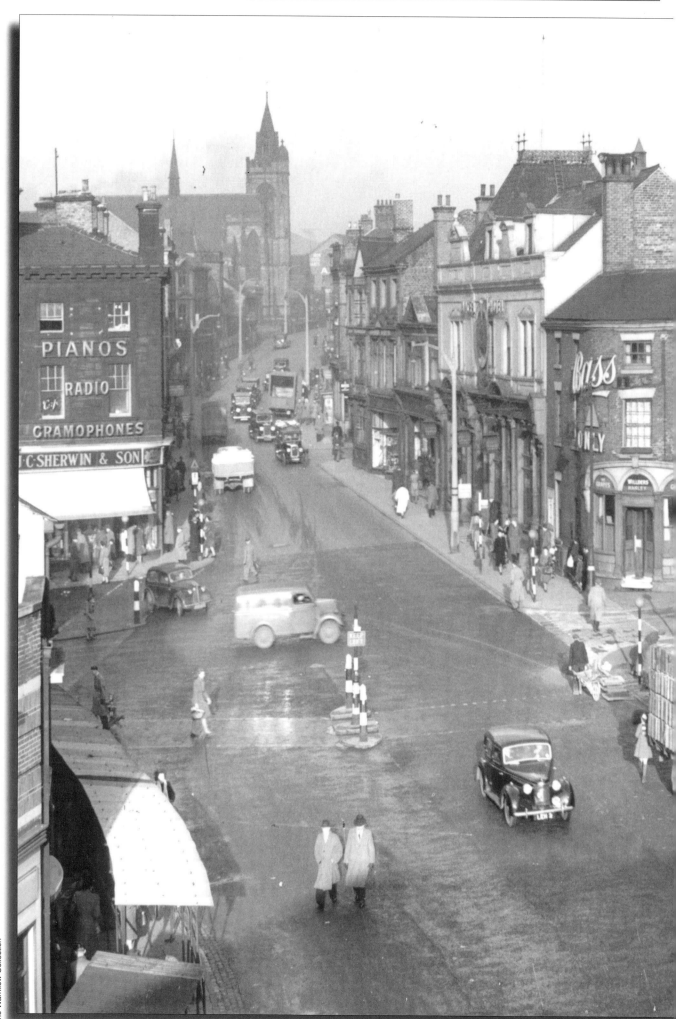

The Warrillow Collection

Left: It takes you back, doesn't it? This was Hanley High Street as it was in 1948, now of course Town Road that takes you out towards Hanley Forest Park. The streets were quiet when the photographer captured this nostalgic scene, and vans and delivery wagons make up the biggest part of the traffic.

It seems strange now to see the city centre without the ubiquitous double yellow lines, one-way streets and pedestrian precincts. But there was little traffic about in 1948; most of the cars in use were pre-war; though the war had been over for three years goods were still in short supply, and this included new cars. At that time private cars were still widely regarded as being pretty much a middle-class commodity, and the people of Stoke-on-Trent had some way to go before post war prosperity was in their grasp and the ordinary person in the street could afford to buy a family car.

This part of the city has been changed for ever. The Grapes Hotel and the Angel Hotel on the right have gone along with Swinnerton's Café on the left, where you might have met a friend met for lunch, and Sherwin's music store next door.

Above: Colourful flowerbeds on the roundabout brightened the scene for the local inhabitants of Stoke back in 1960. Looking along Glebe Street from Church Street, Stoke, the Town Hall can just be picked out on the left. St Peter's is the lovely old church on the right. Built to a Trubshaw and Johnson's design in 1830, the Perpendicular style church was the 'mother church' that served the largest part of the city until the early years of the 19th Century. The old Stoke Church that preceded it was demolished in 1826, and construction work began on the new building during the same year. The old cemetery can number some famous names among its inhabitants; Josiah Wedgwood, Josiah Spode and Thomas Minton are all buried there.

Today Stoke is the home of the Spode Museum and Visitor Centre and the Minton and Portmeirion Factory Shops.

Right: Until the middle of the 18th Century Burslem was a small moorland village - a fact which seems hard to believe on looking at this rooftop scene. Developments that came about as a result of the Industrial Revolution, together with improved local communications led to the rapid growth of the town. The date of this photograph is unknown, but Burslem was by that time obviously dominated by industry; the view is peppered with factory chimneys and bottle ovens, and spoil heaps turn the far horizon into a scene straight from the Valley of the Kings.

Josiah Wedgwood, probably Burslem's most famous son, was born in the town in 1730, and the Wedgwood Memorial Institute was built to commemorate the master potter's achievements. A shrewd businessman as well as a skilful innovator, Wedgwood put his stamp of high quality on the wide range of wares that left his factory. The foundation stone of the Wedgwood Institute was laid by William Gladstone, and along with other buildings in the area it featured in one of Arnold Bennett's novels.

Bennett died in 1931 and his ashes were interred in Burslem Cemetery.

Inset: The old Port Vale ground dominates this hilltop view of industrial Hanley, with its many pot banks and the spoil heap on the horizon - a very different place back in 1950 when this photograph was taken to the city we are familiar with today. Over the years the Club saw a number of name changes; the Club was formed back in 1876 as Port Vale Football Club, and on moving to Burslem in 1884 they became Burslem Port Vale. The Club moved to the recreation ground in Hanley in 1913, dropping 'Burslem' from their name.

Port Vale have fought their way through many difficult periods in their long history, but to their credit have always bounced back. Relegated for the first time in 1928-29, the Club responded by winning the Third Division (North) Championship, attaining 5th place in Division Two (still the Club's highest league position).

Between 1936 and 1953 the Club fluctuated between Third Divisions North and South. Port Vale left Hanley in 1950 for the Club's present ground at Vale Park in Burslem, leaving the old stands at Hanley to the demolition teams.

The Warrillow Collection

The Warrillow Collection

The Warrillow Collection

Above: *Fountain Square, Hanley, in 1958, and the streets are busy with shoppers. Situated in the centre of Hanley, the Fountain Square area is still a vibrant centre for shopping, eating and entertainment and there is something to suit everyone's taste in the variety of eating houses and pubs in and around the square. The fountain to which the square owes its name no longer runs with water, but at least the old landmark provides a focal point amid the surrounding flower beds.*
The building in the foreground on the far left of the photograph houses the lively and well established pub Ye Olde French Horn, a Bass house whose impressive wall mirror is legendary and definitely deserving of a mention here. A small street market helps to retain the traditional character of the area; a market has been held on the site for centuries, and though many of the stalls moved to the market arcade in the Potteries Shopping Centre at the beginning of the 1990s a number of traders still set up their stalls in the Fountain Square and Market Street area.

Right: *This pigeon's eye view of Hanley gives us a glimpse back in time to the city that no longer exists today. The white building almost in the centre of the photograph is the Potteries Museum which was built on the corner of Bethesda Street and Broad Street in the mid-1950s, occupying the site of the old Bell Pottery. It was only after a 25-year campaign that it was agreed to build the new museum, which cost £46,000. To the right of the museum is the well-known Bethesda Chapel (dubbed 'The Potteries Cathedral'), which was at one time patronised by a significant number of influential citizens of the city. Further to the right is the school; the building still exists, though its use has changed in recent years. The chimneys and bottle ovens along the skyline have now disappeared, leaving St John's church to stand alone. Great swathes of the city have also gone to make room for the Inner Ring Road that now sweeps across the centre of this view, and a whole area of buildings to the left of centre below the horizon were cleared for the building of the Potteries Shopping Centre, completed during the 1980s.*

Below: Tall chimneys punctuate this pigeon's eye view of Stoke as it was in 1947; the photograph was possibly taken either from Hartshill Church or from Penkhull. Until the middle of the 18th Century the church of St Peter and the church buildings that surrounded it was just about all there was to Stoke - most of the population lived in the village of Penkhull. St Peter's, built between 1826 and 1830, is thought to be the church in the background on the right, and you can see a memorial tablet and a relief portrait of Josiah Wedgwood in the chancel.

As one of the areas most noted industrialists, Wedgwood was also given pride of place outside the entrance to Stoke railway station.

The elegant two platform-one-bay Victorian station once had more trains passing through it than any similar station in the country, and thankfully still survives today, having being preserved at a time when towns such as Stafford and Wolverhampton were during the post war years replacing their stations.

Right: The air is heavy with smoke from bottle ovens in this 1950s view of Longton from Normacott Road, and the building whose tall gable end adjoins the white building towards the left is Tams Pottery. The area has seen many changes over the last forty years or so, and the chimneys that jut into the skyline gave way to progress in the form of the bus station - not to mention Jollies Night Club! Longton was the terminus for the first tram service to run between Tunstall, Burslem, Stoke and Longton - the Number 24 route. The tram had seating for 24 passengers, hence the number given to the run, though the journey must have been a tooth-jarring experience. The wooden bench-type seats made no concession to comfort except that the seat backs were adjustable so that passengers could face in the direction the tram was travelling. One of Longton's more famous sons was the musician Havergal Brian, who was born in nearby Dresden in 1876. Brian was a child prodigy whose skills were largely self-taught. He lived to see his Gothic Symphony performed at the Royal Albert Hall under Sir Adrian Boult in 1966; he died six years later in 1972.

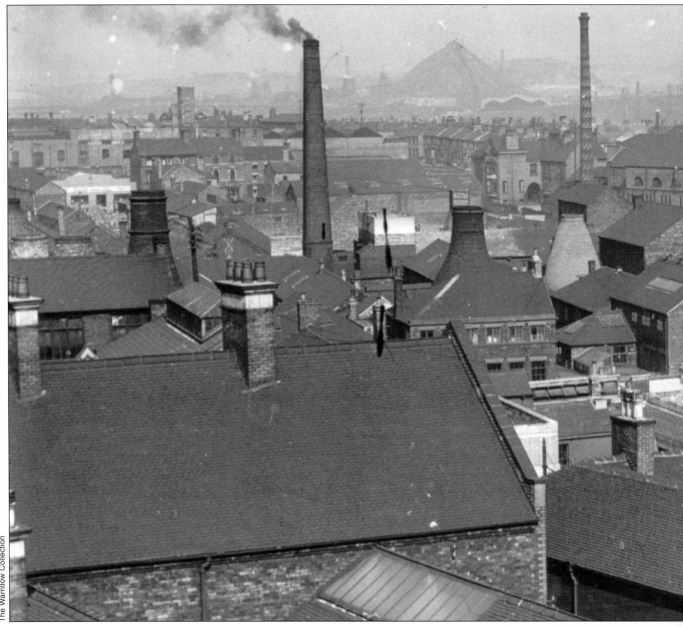

This busy scene in Campbell Place in Stoke was captured on camera in 1956 - familiar to many of our readers who will perhaps have bought their jacket and trousers at Burton's Tailors on the right of the picture, or partaken of a pint or three of the right stuff at the Talbot hotel further along on the left. One of the details of the photograph that quickly catches the eye is of course that the motor cyclist crossing the junction is not wearing a crash helmet. Far less attention to the safety of motorists and motor cyclists was paid forty years ago than today, when the wearing of seatbelts and approved safety helmets is obligatory.

Readers will just be able to pick out the Spode factory in the background on the right. Josiah Spode first established his porcelain and pottery business in 1770 and the firm is still operating today. In its earlier days the factory produced creamware, later becoming famous for bone china which was introduced by Spode's son, also named Josiah, in 1794. The firm traded as Copeland and Garrett between 1833 and 1848; the name Spode was revived in 1970.

The Warrillow Collection

The Warrillow Collection

Above: A sad day for the Essoldo in Hanley as a demolition team goes to work on the old building. It was 1962, and over the past decade the rising popularity of television had been making inroads into cinema audiences all across the country. During the 1930s and 40s The Palace, as the cinema was at that time, was extremely popular. When attendances began to wane the management of the Essoldo tried everything; they screened all the great musicals such as 'Carousel' and 'The King and I', and in 1960 while 'Gigi' was on the programme they employed Nanette, a female organist who charmed the audiences with her playing during the intervals. But the size of the establishment had become a distinct drawback, and it was increasingly difficult to fill the vast auditorium.

The Essoldo, built in the early years of the 20th Century on Stafford Street and Cheapside,

closed its doors for the last time in May 1962. The last programme included two X-rated films, 'Naked as Nature Intended' and 'Call Girl Business'. A modern building, which included a Bingo Hall, was erected on the site of the old cinema.

Top: The impressive classical facade of the Town Hall dominates this scene of Burslem Market Place and St John's Square. In the right foreground stands the lovely old drinking fountain topped by a lamp supported by two intertwined dolphins. The corner of Jenkins Street near the Town Hall was the site of the Burslem Theatre Royal; built around the turn of the century, it was also known as the Wedgwood Theatre. In 1911 the old theatre was demolished and was replaced by the new Queen's Theatre Hall.

The Old Burslem Borough Police Station was at one time situated behind the Town Hall, from where the local force could keep a weather eye on what was going on in the town centre. They often had need to. Burslem Market Place has seen a great deal of life over the years. In earlier years the market square had stands for four hackney carriages, and one of the drivers, Fred Hall, made himself unpopular with the local constables (not to mention the other drivers) by refusing to obey the local by-laws on where his cab was allowed to stand for hire, choosing instead to go where the business was better.

Three separate photographs from the early 1940s have been combined to make this view of Stafford Street in Hanley. Readers will have many fond memories of shopping at Lewis's - the building on the left with the clock. Do you remember the food hall window on Stafford Street that was piled high with ring doughnuts every Saturday? And taking the children along to see Santa Claus in his grotto at Christmas? The cash room known as the 'tube room' was a feature peculiar to Lewis's; money from departments without a till was sent to the tube room where the assistant on duty, meticulously dressed in black and white, took the cash and gave out the change. Lewis's acquired the building that fronted Stafford Street and Miles Bank in 1935 at a cost of £250,000, and the department store remained a favourite with shoppers for many years. Many of the buildings in the centre of this photograph were cleared for the new Potteries Shopping Centre, opened in the late 1980s. The streets to the right are pedestrian shopping precincts today, while Stafford Street is part of the city's one-way system.

Left: The date given for this photograph is 1943, and this is Hanley as the Luftwaffe would have seen it. During World War II Stoke-on-Trent was not a prime target for enemy bombs; in the North and the Midlands the heaviest raids were reserved for cities such as Coventry, Sheffield, Manchester and Liverpool. The city did have its bombing raids, however, as some older readers will remember. Houses in May Bank and around the city were hit by stray clusters of bombs in 1941, and the new nurses' home at North Staffordshire Royal Infirmary was targeted. Shelton Bar Steelworks also suffered, as did the Wedgwood factory at Etruria. St John's church is a landmark to look for in this aerial view, just off-centre towards the top of the picture. Many of the nearby blocks of buildings were demolished when the city centre was redeveloped during the late 1980s. The distinctive rooftops of the Tontine meat market can be seen almost in the centre of the photograph; the school in the left foreground was demolished together with much of the nearby shopping area to make way for the new bus station.

Above: Many readers will remember buying their Sunday roast in the meat market in Burslem, demolished in the 1950s.

The site of the old market, however, brought television fame to Burslem during 1998 when a team of archaeologists converged on the car park and the landscaped area, making it the focus of their search for the remains of Josiah Wedgwood's first kiln. The team were in the city as part of the popular 'Time Team' programme, a 'viewer friendly' weekly archaeology show that goes out on Channel Four during certain months of the year. 'Time Team' features 'Blackadder' actor Tony Robinson when he is not being Baldrick - at first it was difficult for viewers to accept the actor's other, more serious, side!

The dig took place in June, and five trenches were dug on the site; though the foundations of an old kiln that dated from around 1800 were found, the team were disappointed in their search for the foundations of the actual Wedgwood kiln. The dig was far from a failure, however, as a number of pieces of pottery that were contemporary with Wedgwood were discovered.

At leisure

Below: Young boys play their own half-hearted game of cricket while keeping more than half an eye on how the real game is progressing on the other side of the playing fields.

The Shelton Bar Steelworks provides a rather grim backdrop to this thought-provoking 1950s photograph, reminding us that not too many years ago industry of one kind or another greeted us at every turn and destructive pollution clouded the air. By the late 1800s respiratory disease was the major cause of death in the area, and the value of open spaces around the six towns was recognised. Public parks and recreation grounds were established; these playing fields at Etruria that also provided a children's playground were one of the smaller parks in the area.

Queen's Park, the first public park in the Potteries, was opened in July 1888 in Longton on land donated by the Duke of Sutherland. In the 1890s 80 acres of derelict land at Hanley was landscaped and turned into a public park with an ornamental boating lake. Each of the six towns laid down parks - apart from Stoke, whose town councillors argued that Hanley Park was near enough for its citizens to use.

Right: This memorable photograph was taken during the Capitol Cinema's final programme before its closure in 1963, when 'Donovan's Reef' starring John Wayne was screened. The cinema in Goodson Street, Hanley, had a long history and several changes of names in its lifetime. It began providing entertainment in Hanley in the late 1890s as the Alexandra Music Hall, after which it became the Gaiety, then the Empire, and after that The Kings Palace Theatre. Short films were introduced, and as moving pictures gained in popularity they gradually took over from live theatre. The facility became the Capitol in August 1925, opening with the film 'Kalora - the Belle of the Orient'. In earlier years the cinema had its own orchestra, and Jack Moss and the Capitolists were the cinema's resident players. The 1940s and 50s saw a boom in the popularity of the cinema, and long queues would herald each performance. During the war cinema newsreels kept the people visually in touch with what was happening, though propaganda and censorship prevented the entire story from being told. Cinema provided the ordinary working person with a cheap and enjoyable night out; in 1952 a seat in the front stalls only cost 1/6d.

Chairoplanes, roundabouts, dodgem cars, sideshows - they were all there in the park and in the streets of Hanley. Wakes week had an atmosphere of its very own that had to be experienced to be appreciated. The whirr and hum of the rides, the loud beat of the music, several different tunes fighting with each other for attention, the squeals of the girls as they whirled and spun. And the food! The shocking pink candy floss that was spun around a stick while you waited, the toffee apples, dark red and shining as if they had been varnished, and the paper bags of crunchy brandy snap and the ice cream, in tubs, cornets or wafers. Weeks in advance the local children were eagerly awaiting the wakes week festivities which were held in each town around the Potteries, especially those stay-at-homes who could not get away for a week at the seaside. The wakes fair was their holiday, and they loved it.

During the 1870s an attempt was made to co-ordinate the wakes celebrations, but little came of it. People preferred to attend their own fair - then have the pleasure of attending others elsewhere!

THE NEW ROXY

GLASS ST., HANLEY.
(LATE THE IMPERIAL).
Phone 5497 HANLEY.   Licensed: J. PICKLER.

| COMFORT | | Perfect Sound |

SPECIAL HOLIDAY ATTRACTION

WEEK COMMENCING **MONDAY, Mar. 28th**

ALL THE WEEK
THE SCREEN'S GREATEST COMEDIANS

WHEELER & WOOLSEY
in

CUCKOOS

Music   Colour   Singing   Dancing
The Finest Comedy since Pictures started Talking.
IT'S A SCREAM — IT'S A YELL.

MICKEY MOUSE in GORILLA MYSTERY
AND
FULL SUPPORTING PROGRAMME

Please Note : BARGAIN MATINEES DAILY
Continuous from 2-30 to 10-45 Daily
Doors open at 2 o'clock

	SATURDAY
PRICES :	
4d. 6d. & 1/-	6d. 9d. & 1/-

Special Children's Matinee on Saturday at 2 o'clock
Don't miss our Serial on Thursday.

Left: The smell of sawdust and the roars of the crowd once drew local pleasure-seekers to the New Roxy in Hanley to see the Royal Imperial Circus. A skating rink was also part of the building's colourful past, as was Rogers' and Warrilow's People's Music Hall.

The hall became the Imperial Picture Palace in 1913 when a Mr Salt was the owner. But it was Harry Buxton, who held the lease in 1931, who was responsible for the name of the new cinema he opened. Impressed by New York's Roxy Cinema which was the largest cinema ever built, he named the new facility the New Roxy.

Harry Buxton was a flamboyant character with very definite ideas about marketing. He decided to advertise for people to write a slogan for the New Roxy (the winner was 'Rock your cares away in Roxy chairs'), and he paid a prominent actress, Dodo Watts, to ride through the streets in a carriage to announce the opening of the new cinema.

When the cinema closed in 1961 it was converted into a night club, but came to a sad end in 1977 when fire swept through the building.

Above: Do you remember the 'good old days' when Piccadilly in Hanley was known locally as 'the monkey run'? Those were the days when boys strolling down the street would be quite likely to meet up with girls strolling down the street; one or the other would strike up a conversation and if the vibes were right the two of them would adjourn to the nearest milk bar or café for a milk shake or a cup of coffee. More than a few lasting relationships were formed, and a number of elderly couples around Hanley could no doubt testify to the effectiveness of the monkey run as they celebrate their Golden Wedding Anniversaries!

Weren't youthful pastimes a lot more innocent and uncomplicated in those days? The Globe Café in Piccadilly (with Cadbury's hot chocolate on the menu) was no doubt one of the establishments patronised by the teenagers. Between the 1930s and the 1960s Swinnertons turned their café into a Milk bar, then back again to bring their popular café full circle.

The Warrillow Collection

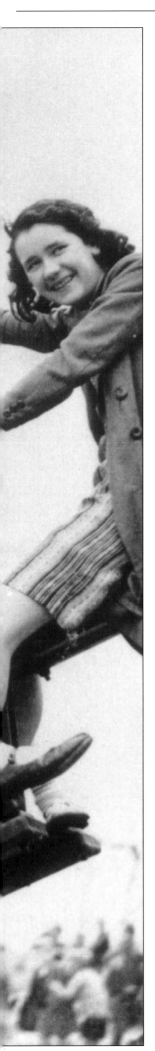

> **PREFABS PRESENTED A QUICKLY-BUILT SOLUTION, AND WHOLE ESTATES OF THEM WERE BUILT AROUND THE COUNTRY**

Left: A world away from the storm clouds of war, the camera catches wide smiles of genuine enjoyment on the faces among this crowd of children - mostly girls - on a swing. The year was 1940, and pleasures were more simple back then than they are now. A day out with the family today almost always involves spending a good deal of money, and children expect to be given expensive toys such as computers and the games that go with them. The children pictured here will no doubt have played with whips and tops, Dinky cars and skipping ropes and used old tyres for hoops. Their games would have been cowboys and Indians (even the girls!), hide and seek and catch.

There was a large crowd in the park the day this photograph was taken, which would perhaps indicate that it was taken during wakes week, the annual holiday everybody looked forward to. During the war years more families would have had stay-at-home holidays because of the difficulties of travelling.

Above: A sunny day in Cobridge, and these young girls are the only signs of life in a virtually traffic free street. Back in 1960, when this photograph was taken, the traffic flow was obviously significantly less than it is today!

Do you remember prefabs? They were still part of the Cobridge landscape in the 1960s. The lack of sufficient housing had become a real problem in most large towns and cities during the 1920s and 1930s. Many young couples were having to live with in-laws and many districts were overcrowded; large new estates such as those built in Trent Vale in 1929 by the Sutton Housing Trust were built around the six towns. Prefabs presented a quickly-built solution, and whole estates of them were built around the country to offer temporary housing. People from older properties were used to doing without bathrooms and using outside toilets, and the surprisingly spacious little bungalows with bathrooms, separate toilets, and modern kitchens quickly became popular. Prefabs lasted far longer than had been intended, but they were gradually phased out and replaced by new housing estates.

The Warrillow Collection

Above: Can you believe that it's nearly 40 years since the Gaumont at Burslem closed down? When the last film was screened in November 1960, the Gaumont - originally a music hall called The Coliseum Theatre of Varieties - had been entertaining the local populace since 1914. That was the year the first world war started, and The Coliseum's first recorded show was a concert for soldiers and sailors. The theatre was built with almost 1800 seats that were very often filled, which goes to demonstrate the popularity of music hall back then. Amusements were few at that time; there was the public house, the piano in the living room, the bandstand in the park and not much else for the ordinary person in the street, and music hall provided a unique kind of entertainment that proved to be extremely popular. 'The Col' gradually began to show films and in 1929 Gaumont British Picture Corporation took over the theatre.

This photograph was taken during the Gaumont's final week; the cinema's last programme was a double bill of fare - 'Too Many Crooks' and 'Bachelor of Hearts' - then 'That's your flippin' lot, cock,' a huge notice in the foyer told the cinema's last audiences.

Right: The fields around Etruria were the playground of many local children, and playing with the biscuit ware dumped on the Horse Fields was one of their favourite pastimes. This industrial scene - and the boys who played there that day - was taken from Hartshill. What happened to them all, and what kind of lives did they carve out for themselves?

By the time Josiah Wedgwood set up in the ceramics business in 1759 the area was already producing a wide variety of pottery and had begun the change to a factory industry from the original cottage-based industry. Using his birthplace as a base, Wedgwood bought the Ridge House estate in the Fowlea Valley, which was earmarked as part of the route of the new Trent and Mersey Canal. On its bank, at the point where the turnpike road crossed it, he built what was destined to be one of the largest factories in Britain, later adding rows of model cottages along the turnpike road for the workers. He renamed the settlement Etruria in honour of an ancient pottery design. The factory, along with much of the village, has now been demolished.

The Warrillow Collection

Below: An air of desolation and decay hangs over the old Port Vale stands as the demolition team move in with crane and lifting gear. After playing at the recreation ground in Hanley for 37 years, the Club had moved on to Vale Park (dubbed 'the Wembley of the North') in 1950. Just a couple of years later the Club were celebrating their best season ever as in 1953-54 they romped into the Third Division (North) Championship while at the same time reaching the FA Cup semi-finals. After a two-year stay in Division Two, they went down in 1957 into the newly formed Fourth Division. A record 110 goals turned the season into a success.

The Club reached the fifth round of the FA Cup in 1960 and 1962, while 1963 and 1964 saw fourth round matches. A turn of fortunes in 1965 meant relegation once more to Division Four, while in 1968 the Club found themselves in the unfortunate position of having to seek re-election. The next few years were unproductive and it was not until 1988-89 that a major turning point was reached and promotion via the play-offs carried the Club back to Division Two - a high point in the Club's chequered history.

JOSIAH WEDGWOOD CUT THE FIRST TURF OF THE TRENT & MERSEY CANAL ON 26TH JULY 1766

Right: The compleat anglers....but did they catch anything? There will be more than one reader who will remember their own youth, when they spent Saturdays and school holidays doing exactly the same thing. Playing out was far safer back then, and entertainment was not linked to computer games and television. These lads fishing from the banks of the Etruria canal were caught on camera back in 1954. Today the boys will be well past 50; will they recognise themselves and remember that day? The canal has been part of our landscape for our entire lives, and we can scarcely imagine the countryside without it. But before the canal was even conceived the pottery industry was well advanced, and in the 18th Century the roads were atrociously bad and communication was very slow - Macadam's new road surfaces were not introduced to the vast majority of Britain's roads until 1827. Josiah Wedgwood was among those locally who recognised that a canal was necessary if the potteries were to open up a national - and hopefully international - market. He himself cut the first turf of the Trent and Mersey Canal on 26th July 1766, though the canal was to take eleven years to complete.

The Warrillow Collection

Bolted to the needs of industry
The story of a local firm that grew from two men to a staff of 280

In 1963, an ambitious entrepreneur and his partner were offered two garages in Waterloo Road, Cobridge, at a greatly reduced rent. They seized them gratefully and in that somewhat humble setting established a business which, in the course of 35 years, has matured into one of the Midlands' best known names in engineering supplies.

quantities and a small number of sizes. Furthermore, they were generally supplied in one or two hundred-weight hessian sacks and had to be moved by hand on sacktrucks - a dirty, oily, unpopular job. Mr Key realised that an excellent opportunity existed for a company that could supply a wide range of fasteners in all shapes and sizes, providing a specialised service to industry. In the long term it was clear there would be further market potential in related ranges, such as tools and pipeline products. No other company was offering such a wide-ranging, specialised service which addressed the needs of industry so discriminatingly. FWB was born.

FWB Products Ltd was the brainchild of Mr Henry John Key. Born into a farming family in Newcastle-under-Lyme, he had spent some years in the RAF before joining the costings office of the Midlands Electricity Board and later worked for James and Tatton (the steel stockholders), rising through the ranks to become Sales Representative. By the early 1960s he had accumulated broad-based experience in a variety of roles - but more to the point he had spotted a gap in the market and was eager to fill it. It all came down to nuts and bolts...

A number of companies sold fasteners to local industry but, Mr Key discovered, only in limited

The first task for the new business was to acquire adequate stocks of fasteners of the right quality. Mr Key was determined that, from the outset, FWB's

Above: An old view of Whieldon Road with Whieldon Sanitary Potteries in the foreground, in front of what is now FWB's site. Below: The original single-storey building on Whieldon Road in 1967.

name would be synonymous with the very highest standards of product and service. This proved an immediate challenge for the fledgling enterprise - Britain's manufacturing capacity was still struggling to recover from the effects of the war and demand was fierce - but at last, appropriate supplies were found. One night in July 1963 the first delivery of bolts and nuts, five tons in all, arrived at Mr Key's home. His wife, although heavily pregnant pitched in and helped in the laborious process of counting every one out. Before long, however, she was involved in labour of a very different sort: at around five the next morning she gave birth to their first son, Antony!

In the early days of FWB, Mr Key and his colleague did all the work themselves, sometimes staying up all night to assemble orders. By 1964 they were able to take on one employee, and thereafter additional members of staff as the business began to take off, but flexibility and long hours remained the order of the day (and night!) for the next five years. The company's catchment area stretched from Chester and Shrewsbury in the West, through Staffordshire, to Derbyshire in the East. It was not unusual for Mr Key to collect an order from Bishop's Castle (Shropshire) in the afternoon, return with it to Stoke late that evening, compile the customer's order then leave again at dawn to ensure its delivery in the morning. He regularly put in 90 hours a week throughout this period, whilst the company's growing personnel became used to turning their hand to anything. One winter's day a client arrived for a meeting in FWB's Sales Office and paused outside to commiserate with a

Top: Extensive stocks in the late sixties. *Right:* The height of weighing technology, 1967.

snow-covered workman, struggling in the cold to unload stock from a wagon. 'Ooh, I feel sorry for you lot,' he said, 'having to work outside on a day like today.' And he went inside to wait in the warmth of the office. Moments later, he was joined by the man he was due to meet - Chris Hatchell (a future director of FWB) - who was covered in snow and had to wash his freezing hands because (you've guessed it) they were covered in oil and muck from unloading that wagon. Such was the versatility of FWB staff in the early days.

Meanwhile, the partner's wives provided unstinting, loving support despite the long hours worked by their menfolk. It is, after all, in the nature of a small business, if it is to succeed, that it demands a phenomenal commitment of time and energy from all concerned; inevitably that includes the entire family - everyone pulling their weight towards a common end.

After four years, the company, now with 10 employees, had outgrown its two garages and was able to move to a site on Whieldon Road where a purpose-built single storey warehouse, furnished with ex-government surplus racking, provided ample accommodation for the 300 tons or so of stock that were now held. On-site office space completed the building work. FWB was beginning to reward its hard-working partners and staff. In fact, Whieldon Road remains the company's headquarters even today - a testament to Mr Key's far-sighted planning over 30 years ago.

It wasn't long before the business expanded and the product range extended, just as Mr Key had anticipated. By 1969, FWB Products Ltd consisted of a Tools Department, a Bolts and Nuts Department, and a Pipes and Fittings Department (with a tube warehouse added later). By 1971 an office block had been constructed and there were between 50 and 60 people employed by the company.

Top left: The first FWB trade counter, 1969. Left: The FWB Tools department office in the late seventies.

In 1970 FWB made its first foray into acquisitions, purchasing a small tools company in Wales. The business did well and in 1976 relocated to purpose-built premises on the Coedpoeth Industrial Estate, just outside Wrexham where it established itself as FWB Cymru Ltd.

FWB itself was by now well established, but continued to grow as a result of a

Right: The FWB Tools and Pipeline trade counters in the late seventies.
Above: Stock control before the days of computerisation, 1971.

progressive and proactive regime in garnering customers together with an impressive reputation for quality and service.

Mr Key worked hard to gain an account with De Havilland (now British Aerospace) and to that end cultivated useful personal contact with their buyers - to such an extent that he found himself playing regular games of dominoes with them during Wednesday lunchtimes! Needless to say, he took care never actually to win a game.

On another occasion, just as Mr Key was leaving the Whieldon premises for the night, a desperate - but unfamiliar - customer rushed in with a broken rubber ring from a vacuum cleaner. Please could they help? He had promised his wife that he would buy a replacement, but it had completely slipped his mind and now the shop was shut and what was he going to do? Mr Key and another director, Trevor Jackson, pondered the problem. It wasn't a standard product for FWB, but perhaps... They searched out some rubber from the warehouse and in three quarters of an hour had fashioned a perfectly serviceable replacement. The customer was thrilled. And just before he left, he introduced himself as the Chief Purchasing Officer for

Top left: The FWB steel tube warehouse and loading bay circa 1979. *Left:* Modern technology 1970s style.

Left: Mr Key (left) demonstrates a woodworking machine to Councillor Harry Oakes, the Lord Mayor of Stoke-on-Trent, 1986-87. Below: An invitation to the open days in 1971. Bottom: A new FWB vehicle in 1986.

Birmingham and Tamworth to form FWB Withers. But perhaps the most ambitious step, geographically, took place in 1991 with the establishment of FWB South West in Truro, Cornwall.

On a less direct basis, FWB can even claim to have had some influence in Africa. An African student approached the company looking for work experience during holidays from his business studies course at Wolverhampton College. He became a familiar presence at FWB and gained in-depth experience of how to run a successful business. After completing the course at Wolverhampton, he returned home to set up his own African version of FWB.

a major company. He was impressed by the level of service, and some business came FWB's way as a result.

Good customer relations have always been valued at FWB and were instrumental in assuring the runaway success of its first trade exhibition in 1971. Suppliers set up exhibition stalls on FWB premises and a throng of customers arrived, by invitation, to inspect the wide product range offered by the company. 3,000 visitors were made welcome over three days, exceeding all expectations and putting severe strain on the Directors' and Managers' wives who had gamely agreed to take care of the catering! Subsequently, there were similar, and always popular, exhibitions at five-yearly intervals - although the wives were mightily relieved when professional caterers were brought in to replace them on butty duty.

After the success of the Wrexham operation, FWB moved further afield in the 1980s when it set up a subsidiary company - FWB Peach - in Liverpool, on the banks of the Mersey. In 1990, there was additional expansion when the company took over an engineers' merchants with branches in

FWB's winning formula in Stoke has been applied to all its UK enterprises and generated a dramatic increase in customer base combined with an impressive reputation for targeting industries' particular needs in different locales.

Today, the company's chief markets in the UK are engineering and manufacturing concerns. It also exports to British civil engineering and construction companies working abroad. The product range is diverse and comprehensive, embracing tools and equipment, pipeline, process controls, safety equipment and workwear, and - of course - fasteners. A staggering 50,000 separate line items are now held in stock at the Stoke-on-Trent site. What makes a winning formula? Much of FWB's success comes from its innovative approach in the matter of 'single-sourcing'. Single-sourcing is a process by which a buyer - frequently snowed under by administration dealing with a large base of suppliers, all hungrily competing for business - aims to have a few or even just one very reliable supplier who knows his business well, is responsive to his specific product needs, and who can readily deliver to his precise requirements, cost-effectively, and at a consistent quality. FWB, with its vast product range, is well placed to develop this mutually beneficial arrangement with its customers, but it goes further: offering to act as buying agents for items that are not part of its standard product range, and tailoring order-receiving, deliveries and invoicing to suit individual customers' preferences. Customers like it,

and are turning in increasing numbers to FWB as their sole supplier of engineering and safety goods. In factories and workshops there's a common refrain: 'FWB will have it'. And inevitably, they will. More to the point, the quality is guaranteed. FWB purchases and stocks only products that meet stringent British, American or European Standards.

Mr Key also takes pride in the top-notch service his friendly,

Top: The modern premises as they are today. Left: FWB sponsored the Eastwood Football Club team for a number of seasons.

Whieldon Road's Industrial Estate - funded almost entirely by Mr Key. He had bought the 1902 timepiece (which graced Pye Hill pit in Nottinghamshire until the 1980s) in 1994, when the Chatterly Whitfield Mining Museum closed and auctioned off its artifacts. The clock had played a very important part in life around Pye Hill - a landmark and important reference point not only for miners but for other workers in the locality, and for children on their way to and from school. Mr Key determined that it should have a similar role today and provided for the construction of the impressive brick clock tower in its new home. And there it stands. A testament to the abiding legacy of industry and its modern place in the world.

FWB has come a long way since those lock-up garage days of 1963. It now employs 150 people in Stoke-on-Trent alone, has four subsidiary companies, and boasts the very latest computer technology and materials-handling equipment. Yet the underlying philosophy remains as palpable now as it was at the very beginning: to look after the customer's needs and to offer the very highest levels of service.

Top: An aerial photograph of FWB taken in 1994.
Left: The Pye Hill Clock and clock tower on Whieldon Road's Industrial Estate, pictured in December 1995, shortly after completion. Below: FWB Chairman and founder Mr Key (standing), with, from left to right, his son Antony, his wife Betty, son Andrew and daughter Josephine.

highly trained staff are able to provide. Regular training sessions ensure that FWB employees are abreast of developments across the full spectrum of product lines, and can offer professional and up-to-the-minute advice to all their customers.

If business is about anything, it's about serving the needs of people and Mr Key has always kept this as a primary objective - looking after his customers and his staff in exemplary fashion. But his commitment to the community at large goes further: He served for 21 years as a JP and for seven years was International chairman of Longton Rotary Club. He has also devoted much time and energy, on the finance committee and as deputy chairman, to the YMCA and, in a reminder of his roots, acted as President of the Staffordshire Agricultural Society for a term. His interest in cultural opportunities for young people is well known and bore fruit for many local youngsters when FWB became sponsor of the bi-annual Stoke-on-Trent Young Musician of the Year competition. The nursery classroom at St Werburg's Primary School owes its existence to a generous contribution from Mr Key.

1995 saw the Lord Mayor of Stoke-on-Trent unveiling the Pye Hill Clock and clock tower on

On the home front

Left: Throughout World War II the Theatre Royal in Hanley survived the Luftwaffe unscathed - only to be almost totally destroyed by a fire that swept through the well-loved cinema on 2nd June 1949, leaving only the rear wall of the building intact.

Originally the Royal Potteries Theatre, the entertainment hall was opened in 1841 and over the next 50 years or so went through various stages of redesign and rebuilding. The first cinematograph licence was granted in 1916 to C Elphinstone to show films for a period of three weeks during a live variety performance. As the Theatre Royal the hall began to show films in 1922 just in time to captivate its audiences with 'Little Lord Fauntleroy' which starred Mary Pickford as the engaging but over-innocent little Cedric's mother. Like a phoenix from the ashes, a new Theatre Royal was constructed on the site of the old. Designed by Forshaw and Greaves, the new theatre was opened on the 14th August 1951. The rising popularity of television spelled the end for many cinemas, and little more than a decade on the Theatre Royal became a Bingo hall before reverting once more to live theatre during the 1980s.

Below: These young soldiers look remarkably cheerful in spite of being relegated to spud bashing and other kitchen duties; maybe peeling potatoes was preferable to the alternative - whatever that was!

During World War II this company's camp was in Trentham Park, which would indicate that the men were French Legionnaires. They had been transferred to Britain from Norway, where they had fought desperately to repel the invading German army. In 1940 Hitler had invaded Norway; he faced a determined people and a desperate fight but the Allies withdrew during May and June and the Norwegian army were forced to surrender. The Norwegian resistance movement proved to be a thorn in Hitler's side; throughout the rest of the war they continued to harass the German garrison and Hitler had to keep 300,000 soldiers in Norway to counter the resistance. Interestingly it was the Norwegian Campaign that led to the fall of Neville Chamberlain in May 1940; he was succeeded by Winston Churchill who eventually was to lead the British to victory. As leader of the Free French Forces, General de Gaulle visited Stoke-on-Trent during the summer of 1940.

Above: Viewed from the Sneyd Arms, Hanley Road was in the 1920s virtually deserted - a far cry from the same busy road today! Seventy years ago you would have been more likely to travel by public transport than in a car; private cars (which had only been invented a mere 40 years earlier) were at that time still very much a middle class symbol. Even delivery vehicles were still largely horse-drawn, and the milkman and the coalman would probably have been using a horse and cart well into the 1940s.

The houses look familiar, but the gas lamp (with arms to take the lamplighter's ladder!) and the distinctive telegraph poles as well as the lovely old car remind us of the age of this photograph. The residents who occupied these council houses were the lucky ones; the town unfortunately still had its slum areas where families were crowded together and perhaps a dozen people might have to use the one toilet that stood in the back yard. During the 1920s and 1930s the council embarked on an extensive programme of slum clearance and house building, and huge estates provided thousands of families with mod cons, gardens - and space to breathe.

Right: Rows of chimneys - many of them now gone for ever - jut into the skyline at Shelton Bar steelworks in this dramatic 1960s photograph taken from the top of the rather steep Etruria Vale Road, which connects Etruria with Shelton. The name 'Shelton' which was given to the works is something of a misnomer, as the steelworks were set up some distance from the village of Shelton itself. In its heyday the plant employed 3,000 workers but by the 1950s the area was fast turning into an industrial wasteland. Many attempts were made to attract new industries to Etruria, and in the 1980s Etruria Hall, one-time home of Josiah Wedgwood, was taken over as the headquarters of the National Garden Festival which was held on part of the site of the former Shelton Steelworks. The area has today been regenerated, largely as a trading estate and a leisure facility offering visitors a wide choice of activities. You can now turn a shopping trip into a day out by doing your weekly shop at Morrisons supermarket, eating a burger and fries at McDonald's, then catching a movie at the multi-screen cinema before heading for home at the end of the day.

Events & occasions

Below: The nearby canal provided firefighters with a handy source of water when incendiary bombs fell on the Wedgwood factory in 1941.

A team of firewatchers had been organised at the start of World War II, and the watchers took turns to stay overnight at the factory. Using a bench as a makeshift bed the watchers slept as and when air raid warnings allowed. The incendiaries that hit the works did little damage apart from instantly firing a pug of clay into a solid mass! More damage was done at the Shelton Bar steelworks nearby.

During the war the National Fire Service took on the control of all civic fire brigades, and women as well as men worked for the NFS. On occasions incendiaries had fallen into unattended factories and office blocks and started fires - a two-hour bombing raid on London just after Christmas in 1940 started a total of 1,500 fires, many of them burning unchecked in city centre properties. After that, firewatching became a compulsory duty, and all men between 16 and 60 were called on to organise a fire-watching rota. Later on women between 20 and 45 joined them.

Right: When the King and Queen paid a wartime visit to Stoke-on-Trent it came as a complete surprise to everyone. Thousands would have turned out to cheer the royal couple had they known beforehand about the visit, but during the war strict security measures were needed to protect the nation's leaders. But word soon spread that the royal couple were in the area and they were warmly welcomed at Stoke Station. After a refreshing cup of tea obtained from the WVS mobile canteen the King and Queen watched a parade of Civil Defence Services in Station Square. They then visited Shelton Steelworks where they watched a blast furnace being tapped before going on to tour the Spode factory. During World War II King George and Queen Elizabeth lived and suffered with the people of Britain through the dark days of war. The royal couple showed great courage by staying on in England when they could have been evacuated to safety. They insisted that they be treated like everyone else, even to wartime rationing, and the King was almost relieved when Buckingham Palace was bombed. He felt that he could now identify with his people and look them in the face.

The Warrillow Collection

Above: In an area that had so much heavy industry, many people found that the hobby of gardening and allotment keeping gave them the complete change of scene they needed during evenings and weekends.

The annual Horticultural Fete held in July in Hanley drew large crowds year after year. Often an exhibitor would win a particular section time after time - then perhaps be ousted unexpectedly by a complete outsider! The Mayor appears to have been present at this particular event that probably took place during the early 1940s, though it is a lady who is at the microphone - a visiting celebrity perhaps? The formal hats and suits tell us that this Fete was a far more formal affair than it would be today.

During the 1940s of course allotment gardening was regarded as being vital, and the whole nation was encouraged to 'dig for victory'. In gardens everywhere, potatoes replaced roses and peas and beans were put in instead of delphiniums. Every spare foot of ground - even grass verges - was put to good use to keep the nation fed.

Young women were encouraged to join the Land Army, and countrywide around 90,000 of them responded to the appeal.

Above: Hundreds of spectators turned out to watch the Carnival of Queens that took place in Hanley Park in 1950. Note just how much fashions have changed since then; almost every person in the crowd, men, women and children alike, is wearing a head covering of some kind. Male spectators are sporting anything from a natty panama to a flat cap, while the choice of the ladies and little girls ranges from a simple beret to a broad-brimmed sunhat.

We are not certain who won the competition, but the Carnival of Queens could possibly have been linked with the Miss Stoke-on-Trent competition. This became a popular regular event that was much looked forward to, not only by gorgeous girls hoping for recognition as the most beautiful girl in the Potteries, but by spectators who had an appreciative eye for the ladies. The very first Miss Stoke-on-Trent Pageant was held at Port Vale FC's Hanley ground in 1950 - the same year as this Carnival of Queens - and the winner was Miss Joyce Freeman.

Top: During the second world war Stoke-on-Trent did not figure highly on the Luftwaffe's hit list. Their priority targets were the steelworks, the railways, the sewage system - and damningly, the hospital. Incendiaries caused a certain amount of damage at Shelton Bar steelworks and the Wedgwood factory, and caused severe damage to the new nurse's home (fortunately unoccupied at the time) and an operating theatre at the City General Hospital. Stray clusters of bombs damaged houses in May Bank and around the city.

The WVS mobile canteen pictured here must have been a cheering sight to ARP staff, firemen and rescue workers as they brought relief in the form of a much needed cup of tea and a break to working parties around the city. Here the Mayor poses with his tea-drinking party for a photograph; this was obviously a special occasion - perhaps this mobile canteen was just about to go into service?

When the King and Queen paid a wartime visit to Stoke-on-Trent the Queen made a bee-line for the mobile canteen that stood in front of the North Stafford Hotel, and quaffed a large cup of tea. That must have been a proud day for the WVS workers who served Her Majesty.

It's not clear what the celebration was that brought this whole community together, but the ladies' fashions would suggest the Queen's coronation in 1953. The 'queen' of this occasion is obviously the smiling teenager in the centre of the photograph; are the elegantly-robed tots on her left her attendants? The cowboy outfits among the crowd of revellers tell us that a fancy dress competition had been held, as one had in thousands of street parties that were held all over Britain that day. Perhaps a few people among the crowd would have been able to watch the crowning of the Queen in Westminster Abbey on television; it was the first time the coronation of a British monarch had ever been filmed. Television sets were expensive, however, and though Britain had a television service as early as 1936, few people could afford to buy them - and the range of programmes was very limited anyway. By the 1950s sets were beginning to get cheaper, and the Queen's Coronation presented many families with the ideal reason to buy or rent a TV set. Those who did not simply crowded into the parlours of more fortunate neighbours to watch the event!

Above and top: The seaside towns along the coast of North Wales have long been a second home for thousands of families from the Potteries. From the early years of this century regular day trips have run every spring and summer to the North Wales coast, and families who wanted a longer break booked a week or a fortnight at boarding houses in Prestatyn, Rhyl, Colwyn Bay and Llandudno. Many were treated as friends by the landladies who saw the same families during the same weeks year after year.

Back home, the potteries and factories were all closed for the duration of the holiday period, and the air became relatively clear of smoke.

There was plenty to do, but first of all the beach beckoned, and children with buckets and spades made a beeline along Llandudno promenade and on to the sand to build castles and dig moats that would fill with water as the tide came in. Parents would lounge in a deck chair nearby where they could keep an eye on what the children were doing. Another day they might take a ride on the tram to the top of the Great Orme, or book one of the local coach trips to Conwy, further along the coast, or perhaps inland to Betws-y-Coed and the Swallow Falls. Rainy days presented no problem - amusement arcades, funfairs, shops and the local pubs all presented a welcome change from the realities of working life.

Butlins holiday camp in Pwllheli was another favourite destination, and the simple message 'Hi de Hi!' written on the back of the photograph (top) tells us that this group of Potteries ladies were obviously having a great time there. But who were they, and why is the group made up of mostly ladies? And who were the two good-looking chaps in front? Perhaps these were part of the famed team of redcoats. Unfortunately we will never know. We do know that they intended to get together again - a second message says 'See you next year'.

Above: There is scarcely a face without a genuine smile among these members of the workforce at Wedgwood's Etruria factory. The year was 1930, which meant that they had plenty to smile about, as many of these workers would have been personally involved in the week-long Pageant that was held as part of the Wedgwood Bicentenery celebrations. The ambitious event had a cast of 5,000 local people, and a great many more were involved in other ways. Chapters in the city's history were acted out daily in Hanley Park by the relevant sections of the community -members of the Wedgwood family and employees from Etruria enacted the life and times of Josiah Wedgwood, while free churches and the Labour party acted out the chartist riots and scenes of early transport were illustrated by miners and enginemen.

The Pageant was a national event that attracted national attention and drew vast crowds. There was interest too from above - the R100 airship flew low over the pageant ground in order to get a bird's eye view. The final procession of the cast through the streets of Hanley and Stoke drew such vast crowds that a number of people fainted in the crush.

Right: Little girls play in St John's churchyard in Burslem, happily untroubled by the spirits of the long-departed. The date was July 1958, and by that time this graveyard had become an accepted playground for the local children and youths, and many of them were not as innocent as these young girls - a number of graves were desecrated by vandals.

Along with many other graveyards in the area, St John's presented problems of a very different kind back in the mid-19th Century. At that time disease was rife, and the cause of much of it was the water in the wells around Burslem - the water supply used for drinking, cooking and washing was heavily polluted by water that was percolating into it from the graveyard. The fact that the local graveyards were full to capacity added to the problem. In some places the dead were being buried just six inches or so beneath the surface, and local people found the accompanying smells very distressing. It was clear that something had to be done about the situation and in 1860 a new cemetery opened on the Shelton Hall estate. Others followed later. St John's graveyard was closed to burials in 1881.

BETWEEN 1921 AND 1939 MORE THAN 8,000 COUNCIL HOUSES WERE BUILT IN THE SIX TOWNS

A large section of the community whose homes were on Trent Vale housing estate gathered together for this memorable photograph which obviously marked some special occasion. The occasion and the date have now been forgotten - except by those readers who will perhaps recognise themselves as children who smiled for the camera that day.

The years between the two world wars were significant in Stoke on Trent as regards residential development, and huge investments were made in building new homes. Literally thousands of council houses were constructed around the six towns in places like Bentilee and these homes at Trent Vale, built in 1929 by the Sutton Housing Trust. Between 1921 and 1939 more than 8,000 council houses provided countless families in the area with up to date kitchen facilities and modern bathrooms.

Set alongside the old Victorian housing plans that allowed for a tightly-packed forty to fifty homes per acre, the modern estates of between four and fourteen houses per acre offered families a spacious and healthy environment that was convenient to shops and schools.

Today, however, the sheer size of these housing developments is posing problems such as the large demand for school places and provisions for community welfare.

Above: A scene of intense excitement in Wilding Road, Ford Green, as crowds of people lucky enough to be going on an outing wait to board their coaches, watched (with perhaps a touch of envy?) by friends and neighbours from their doorways and windows. A policeman oversees the whole operation, determined to see that the coaches get away without any mishap. This atmospheric old photograph stirs our curiosity, however, and raises more questions than it answers. Where was this large number of coaches bound for? Was the occasion a day trip, or were the excited travellers heading off for a well-deserved week's holiday in Llandudno or Rhyl? And who were they? Members of a local church or club, perhaps?

In the background, lending a slightly Egyptian air to the picture, is the slag heap of Chatterley Whitfield Colliery. A school lay nearby, and after the tragedy at Aberfan, when a local slag heap collapsed on to the school with a huge loss of life, the Chatterley Whitfield spoil heap was cleared. When the colliery closed the site was turned into a mining museum - unfortunately itself short-lived; the museum closed in turn and its collection of exhibits was sold off.

Above right: Keeping one's feet dry required a good deal of forethought back in the days when Ford Green experienced floods such as this one that occurred in February 1946. This particular flood that turned the main road to Norton-in-the-Moors

The Warrillow Collection

into a boating lake reached as far as the level crossing. A number of residents in the worst hit areas became stranded in the upper rooms of their homes, and a boat from the lake in Tunstall Park was used to rescue them by way of the bedroom windows. Dampness was a fact of life that many householders in the area had long learned to live with, and in fact some of the worst affected homes were in the process of demolition when 'the rains came down and the floods came up' once again. The fact that flooding around the district was obviously a problem even in medieval times is revealed in the place names. Silkmore - originally Selchemore - means 'fen with a drain', and a number of settlements contained the word 'pipe'. Floods like this are happily a thing of the past in Ford Green today, though it took an investment of £18,000 for the building of a culvert to bring the nuisance to an end at last.

The Warrilow Collection

Above: Flags fly outside the Midland Bank in Burslem, possibly for the Queen's Coronation in 1953. Ask any resident of Burslem how to find 'The Big House' and you will immediately be directed to this building, built in 1757 by Thomas and John Wedgwood, which became known for its connection with the Chartist Riots.

The Chartist Movement started up in 1836 to campaign for political reform. Feelings ran high, particularly among working class people, who were concerned about poverty, hunger and the hated workhouses set up by the government. Troops were sent to areas where Chartism had a strong hold, and some leaders found themselves transported for life. The petition was presented to Parliament again in 1842 and when it was again rejected widespread strikes and riots followed. Locally , poor pay was at the top of the agenda, and fired by Chartist leaders such as Thomas Cooper, fighting broke out in Burslem. Supplemented by hundreds of marchers from as far away as Manchester, a huge crowd clashed with the militia. Among them was campaigner Josiah Heapy, who was allegedly throwing stones at the troops; he was shot dead on the steps of The Big House. The authorities returned a verdict of justifiable homicide.

The war was over, and the citizens of Stoke on Trent were tired of bombs, gas masks, the blackout and all the other privations of wartime Britain, and when peace was declared after six long years of war bunting was strung from house to house across every street and patriotic flags flapped gaily in the breeze. Along with the rest of Britain they found the energy to let their hair down and organise Victory Parades, street parties, fireworks displays and bonfires - and this parade of happy children (perhaps from a local school?) and their parents and teachers was repeated everywhere across the length and breadth of Great Britain.

It was Britain's new Prime Minister, Clement Attlee, who brought the nation down from its euphoria with a resounding bump. He gave the country a serious warning that although Britain was once more at peace, there was no likelihood of prosperity for the country in the immediate future. Across the world countries were decimated by war, and there were worldwide food shortages. It would be several more years before people could stop using tinned dried eggs or shop for clothes without counting how many coupons they had.

Above: 'Loyal greetings from Burslem' were addressed to the Queen on the occasion of her coronation back in 1953. Burslem was not alone, of course, in rejoicing in the 'New Elizabethan' age - the Coronation of Queen Elizabeth II was an opportunity for Britons around the country to state their patriotism - and an excuse for a country-wide party. Every town and village made their own plans to deck windows and doorways with red, white and blue garlands, hang bunting across every street, run up the Union Jack from every flagpole and plan street parties for all the local kids. Dances were held, shows were staged, fireworks displays were put on and new songs were composed to celebrate the occasion - perhaps readers will remember 'Let's all be new Elizabethans'? The notice on the right announces that a grand Coronation Banquet was to be held in Burslem. Where was it staged, what was on the menu, and how many people were there? Many readers will still hold fond memories of those celebrations that took place so many years ago.

Above right: It was factories such as those of Wedgwood, Spode and Minton that gave rise to a steady demand for talented artists, and in the mid-18th Century schools of design were set up in Hanley, Stoke, and after a long struggle in Burslem. The date of this photograph is easily pinned down to 1953, and Burslem School of Art (situated near the old meat market) is here seen beautifully decorated for the Queen's Coronation.

When her Majesty the Queen was crowned in a Westminster Abbey service on 2nd June 1953, A mere eight years after the end of World War Two, the nation relaxed for the first time and really went to town on the celebrations that welcomed the Queen to the throne. Each town and city, every village institute and church, held their own event, which could range from a simple street party to a big parade. Flags flew from every available window, bunting was strung across the streets, and every major building in the city was decorated artistically - the School of Art's perhaps more so than others!

On the move

Above: Everyone loved a day out, and the delights of Llandudno topped the popularity charts with local families. This local firm operating during the mid-1920s were advertising a 'long day out', and the charabanc left every day during the summer months at 10.00 am. We can't be certain what time the trippers would return, but having been promised a long day by the sea it was likely to be after dark. The weather looked good for this particular party, and once the charabanc was bowling along the sun and wind would blow any workaday blues away; we must hope, though, that the ladies' hats were safe! The vehicle was convertible, and in the event of rain the fold-down hood would be hastily fixed in place.

Factories in the Potteries closed down during the annual holiday weeks; being free from pollution it was the ideal time to stay at home! Many families, of course, could not afford a holiday, and the occasional day trip or visit to Rudyard Lake was much looked forward to.

It was during the 1920s and 30s that railway links networked the Potteries with North Wales, Blackpool and Southport, and day trips that ran from Stoke railway station frequently saw queues that stretched around the building.

Top: Two photographs combine to make up this charming picture of a party of children about to set off on holiday. Many of the children among the group were convalescing after an illness, which probably accounts for their rather subdued smiles. A second reason could be due to the fact that 70 years or so ago such photographs had to be carefully posed and all the subjects had to keep perfectly still. Children were told to keep an eye on the cameraman and 'watch the birdie'; no birdie existed, of course, but the deception kept every child's attention focused in the right direction.

The notices in the bus windows tell us that the party was en route to the Stoke-on-Trent Children's Convalescent and Holiday Home in Rhyl, and the presence of the Mayor and Mayoress with the party tells us that this was a significant visit. These children would have had few holidays to look forward to - back in the 1920s there was little spare cash about for such treats. The Tunstall, Burslem, Stoke and Longton run was route number 24, a number inherited from the tram service. The number referred to the tram, which had 24 seats, rather than the route.

Colourful bunting flutters gaily in the breeze, and one can almost feel the air of suppressed excitement among the crowds in this Crown Bank scene. The year was 1930, and the occasion was the Wedgwood Pageant. The Wedgwood Pageant was a huge affair held to celebrate the bicentenary of the birth of Josiah Wedgwood. The event was advertised nationally by Thomas Cook, and people came to the Potteries from far and wide to join in the fun - even George Bernard Shaw, who arrived unannounced and joined a queue with the rest of the visitors.

Though events were staged throughout the year, the focus of the celebrations was the pageant that took place daily from the 19th to 24th May. Beginning with the Druids, each day a new chapter was enacted, telling the story of Stoke-on-Trent through to modern times. With a cast of 5,000, everything needed careful coordination, from the hiring of horses and riders to the design of the costumes.

Other entertainments were staged in the evenings, such as a military tattoo, a pottery tableau in which 1,500 workers took part, a children's gymnastics display that involved 3,000 school children, folk dancing, torchlight displays and band concerts.

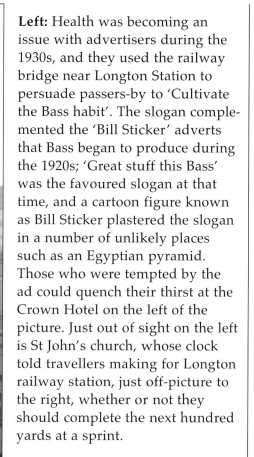

Left: Health was becoming an issue with advertisers during the 1930s, and they used the railway bridge near Longton Station to persuade passers-by to 'Cultivate the Bass habit'. The slogan complemented the 'Bill Sticker' adverts that Bass began to produce during the 1920s; 'Great stuff this Bass' was the favoured slogan at that time, and a cartoon figure known as Bill Sticker plastered the slogan in a number of unlikely places such as an Egyptian pyramid. Those who were tempted by the ad could quench their thirst at the Crown Hotel on the left of the picture. Just out of sight on the left is St John's church, whose clock told travellers making for Longton railway station, just off-picture to the right, whether or not they should complete the next hundred yards at a sprint.

Below: With 2,000 seats on one level and a 30ft wide screen the Palace cinema was reckoned to be the largest in Staffordshire, though for those cinema-goers relegated to the far-off rear seats the size of the establishment was a doubtful privilege. The vast building that was built around 1907 had an interesting history. Originally a wooden roller skating rink, the facility was also the venue for other entertainments such as boxing matches and dances, reflected in its name, the 'Palais de Danse'. A cinematograph licence was granted in May 1921, though its multi-use continued until it closed in 1930. Two years later the Palace Amusements (Hanley) Ltd was created and the company immediately set about carrying out extensive renovations. The old floor was ripped out and replaced, projection facilities were installed, the café was remodelled and a new frontage added. The film 'The Impossible Lover', starring Ramon Navarro, was screened at the grand opening of The Palace on Boxing Day 1932.

In the 1950s the cinema became the Essoldo, and a wide Cinemascope screen with four-track magnetic sound was installed.

Above: There was not a hard hat in sight among these LMS civil engineers supervising the reconstruction work on Scotia Bridge in 1927. 'No hat, no boots, no job' is the slogan that reflects today's emphasis on workers' safety, but 70 years ago employees undertook many dangerous jobs every day without gauntlets, safety glasses, hard hats or protective clothing of any kind, and reflected very little on the risk factor.

The distinctive railway crane, of a type no longer seen today, was there to lift the heavy support beams into place, and the LMS wagons in the right foreground hold the cross members in readiness for the next stage of the building work. The Potteries loop line ran over Scotia Bridge at Tunstall, and around 50 trains a day used the line.

The North Staffordshire Railway had become part of the London, Midland and Scottish Railway Company in December 1922 - but not without a great deal of local controversy.

Right: Another train spotted, and Number 46235 is duly jotted down in these three boys' notebooks as the engine steams noisily by beneath their feet. Then they will look for the next...and the next. A few decades ago thousands of boys (and not a few girls also) took advantage of Stoke-on-Trent's key position on the country's rail network to go train spotting - and a number of our readers were very likely among their number.

Whatever happened to this harmless hobby? The advent of television, video and computer games signalled the demise of many such innocent pastimes, and many of today's railway enthusiasts are in their fifties or sixties. Sadly, a small number of today's youngsters would be more interested in throwing bricks and stones from the bridge as a train passes, or in getting their 'fun' from putting obstacles on the line in an attempt to derail trains. The exact location of this photograph is not known, but the nostalgia is all there: the train spotters, the bridge, the station master, the steam engine. But steam was doomed, and the diesel and electric trains that were introduced across the country in the mid-1950s definitely lacked the character of the old steam engine.

Shopping Spree

Left: It really takes you back, doesn't it? It's amazing just how much nostalgia can be packed into a simple view of the general store at Longport.... Mrs Wellings is the lady standing proudly in the doorway of her shop; her daughter took over the running of the shop in later years. We don't know the date when this lovely old photograph was taken, but the huge Swan Vestas advert together with the lady's clothing lead us to conclude that it was pre-World War II.

Swan Vestas were recommending themselves to smokers as early as 1905 when the slogan 'The smoker's match' was printed on the matchboxes themselves. During the 20s and 30s many adverts stated 'Smokers are requested to use Swan Vestas', but during the second world war the emphasis changed to 'Use matches sparingly' to reflect wartime conditions.

From 1971 advertisers entered into a voluntary agreement with the Department of Health to declare the dangers connected with cigarette smoking, and a warning that cigarettes presented a health risk appeared at the foot of adverts. In 1981 the message 'Cancer cures smoking' really drove the point home - though today's youngsters are still ignoring it in their desire to look cool.

Left: The citizens of Tunstall love a bargain as much as the next person, and an enormous queue of bargain hunters snaked around the corner of the building and down Station Road when Naylor's Bon Marché store in Market Square decided to hold a sale. The date is not known, but the length of the ladies' coats would indicate that the event took place sometime in the 1950s. Naylor's, now converted into a pub, remained for years a popular haunt of shoppers

The old street lights that have bags more character than the today's concrete-post jobs are worth a mention in this memory-stirring photograph.

The Warrillow Collection

Above: Workmen with nerves of steel defy the laws of gravity with little to prevent a fast descent to the pavement below in this dramatic rooftop view of Hanley in 1943. The renovations being done without hard hats were possibly carried out on the roof of the public baths, which were opened in the town in 1874. Hanley church at the top right overlooks a town that is virtually unrecognisable as the same city centre we know today. Many changes have taken place in recent years, not least the number of cars on our city's roads; the sparse traffic along Stafford street contrasts strongly with today's traffic levels. Many readers will no doubt remember buying their shirts, ties and suits at this branch of Burton's gents outfitters. Modern shops replaced this Burton's store in recent years, and the area has now been pedestrianised. The building to the right is the Midland Bank, adjoining George Masons store. The old Lewis's store, built in 1933 at the junction of Miles Bank, Lamb Street and Stafford Street, was demolished in 1964 to make way for new shops. Many other familiar buildings nearby were cleared for the new Potteries Shopping Centre which was completed in the late 1980s.

Above right: A confection in delicate sugar, Queen Elizabeth's elegant state coach leaves Buckingham Palace for her coronation. This delightful display was constructed in 1953 by Mr C P Lester, decorating manager at Swinnertons Bakery, and his team. It is thought that the elaborate display that also included a replica of the imperial crown, the orb and the swords and shield of state, was mounted in a bakery window at Shelton. The eye-catching presentation would have certainly drawn gasps of admiration from passers by.

The pageantry of the occasion is well-remembered by a nation who viewed the coronation on television. The sight of the Queen riding happily back to the palace after the ceremony in the golden State Coach, wearing the crown and carrying the orb and sceptre is one which those who saw it will never forget. Unlike her father King George VI, the young and pretty new queen had begun her training for the throne early, when Edward VIII's abdication in 1936 made her the heir presumptive to the throne. She was only 14 years old when she broadcast messages of encouragement to the children of war-torn Britain, and as the war progressed she gradually took on more and more public duties.

When this nostalgic photograph was taken in 1949, Hanley's well-loved department store Bratt & Dyke already had a long history that went back more than 70 years.

Oliver Bratt and Henry Dyke opened the firm's first store in 1876, and the premises in Trinity Street were built in 1896 on the site of the Roebuck Inn, which was demolished to make way for the new three-storey department store. In the 19th Century it was quite normal practice for shop assistants to live on the store's premises, and the new building provided accommodation for the workforce. Bratt & Dyke laid down strict rules which their workers were obliged to follow; they had to attend church or chapel every Sunday - and were made to take a bath every week! The fact that bathing was obligatory hints that perhaps the workers' accommodation was furnished with a bathroom; if so, the young men and women would enjoy a privilege that few of them would have experienced at home. The Trinity Street store closed its doors for the last time in 1989.

A glimpse back at High Street, Tunstall, and the kind of shops that were characteristic of the 1950s. Leeke's was a typical grocer's shop of the time, where customers would queue to be served and the assistant would weight out butter from a huge slab and slice bacon while you waited - a far cry from today's plastic packs!

The 1950s saw many changes in Britain's shopping habits. The Festival of Britain in 1951 kicked off the new decade, infusing the country with a spirit of new hope, and in 1954 all rationing in Britain was ended, bringing to an end the last of the wartime belt tightening restrictions. Brand names once more appeared on certain food products, and young people were amazed to realise that products such as margarine could be labelled as Stork or Summer County instead of just being plain old foul tasting margarine.

The end of the decade saw the rise of the self service store. The trend started slowly, but it was the thin end of the wedge. Over the last forty or so years there has been a shift towards super- and hyper-markets and out of town shopping.

Below: Today's modern shopping complexes tend to make us forget that shopping centres are nothing new; this nostalgic photograph gives us a glimpse back at covered-in shopping the old style. Lewis's Arcade, pictured here in 1961, was much favoured among the shoppers of Hanley, especially in wet weather! There was little you could not buy at Lewis's - the department store stocked everything from a new dress to half a pound of cheese, and when you had 'shopped till you dropped' you could take the weight off your feet and order a meal or a snack in Lewis's restaurant. Teenagers hanging around the record department stood the chance of bumping into some personality or other; if you were lucky you might have rubbed shoulders with Frank Ifield or Emile Ford. The old arcade, however, had little time left to it - it was demolished three years later. Lewis's new store eventually became as well liked as the old one had been. Debenhams took over the store in 1998.

Bottom: Percy Street in Hanley, and the area is today still recognisable from this photograph that dates from 1958. A modern toilet block replaced the old loos that once stood behind their iron railings in the centre of Crown Bank, and across the alleyway from George Mason's store the Marquis of Granby pub served the local populace with their pints for many years. To the right of the photograph is Fountain Square, today a lively pedestrianised area that benefits from the Potteries Shopping Centre, built during the late 80s. Market stalls are still a feature of the area as they have been for centuries - in fact the old Town Hall was built on the site of the old Butter Market. Opened on 31st July 1845 the Town Hall, which became a branch of Lloyds Bank as early as 1886, was a centre of activity during the Chartist Riots of 1842.

The Warrillow Collection

The Warrillow Collection

A Trading Standards Officer checks the wording on a can in this posed promotional photograph, taken at Siddall's store by the city's Weights and Measures Department in 1960. Siddall & Sons opened two general stores in Fenton in the early years of this Century, and within a few years Siddall's had become a flourishing business. In those early days goods such as biscuits, sugar, dried fruit and salt and pepper were weighed out for the individual customer. People might have to wait a while longer to be served, but at least they had the benefit of personal attention from the staff. But by the mid-1950s self-service was catching on, and a number of local stores including Siddall's made the change. When large supermarkets began to open up and offer goods at cheaper prices, customers naturally shopped where they could save a few shillings. They defected in droves to the self-service super-markets, largely using the corner shop as a standby for bits and pieces they forgot to buy while doing their weekly shop. Gradually many of the smaller businesses found they could no longer compete, and one by one they went to the wall. Siddalls became one of the unfortunate victims.

The Warrillow Collection

and in fact was the largest of the Potteries towns. Today Hanley still has a lot to offer the visitor, offering a bewildering choice of shops and department stores, pubs and clubs, snack bars, fast food establishments and restaurants.

Top: Hanley after dark, and the lighted shop windows reflected in the rain-swept roadway turn the scene into a fairyland. Pictured sometime in the late 60s or early 70s, the Cavendish stores and this branch of the well-

Above: Miles Bank was almost deserted on the day this photograph, taken back in 1960, and there is not a vehicle in sight in Lamb Street. Almost every person in the picture seems to be stepping out briskly with somewhere to go, on their way to work or to school perhaps rather than being in town to browse around the shops. Hanley has long been a thriving centre for shopping and entertainment. As long ago as 1830 it was already described as a large modern town,

known shoe shop chain Dolcis no longer tempt shoppers through their doors. Many of the well-established shops in this area left other firms to take over their premises, and made the move into the Potteries Shopping Centre when the exciting new retail development was built in the city just a few years ago. These quiet roads that during the day were alive with traffic are today part of the city's well-planned pedestrian precincts and one-way traffic system.

At work

Below: A gas lamp lends character to this 1950 photograph taken at the junction of Scotia Road and Williamson Street in Tunstall back in 1950. This was an area of mixed industry; Walter Sylvester Ltd on the left were a motor and general engineering company while on the right are the bottle kilns and chimneys of a neighbouring pottery.

The railway bridge carried the loop line - known affectionately as the 'Knotty' - across the road at this point, which in its heyday was a flourishing concern. By the mid 1950s, however, the sinuous and complicated railway network that linked the pottery towns north of Stoke was fast becoming redundant. The service between Stoke and Kidsgrove at one time numbered more than 70 trains a day; the number was drastically reduced in 1956 and a year later only 16 trains a day halted at Burslem. Attempts made to give the loop line a new lease of life failed, and sections of the disused railway eventually became bridleways, cycle tracks and footpaths.

Right: Two photographs forged into one gives us this cheerful view of the entire workforce of The Variety Wafer Biscuit Co Ltd back in 1936, whose ovens were concerned with biscuit production of a different kind in the Potteries, and whose wafers and cornets were exported to the USA. The occasion for the gathering was to celebrate the transfer of ownership of the factory from Mr Bell, the gentleman wearing a hat seated on the front row, to Mr Foskie, seated on his left. J W Brooks founded the company in 1910 in Hope Street in Hanley, and with the change of ownership came a change of premises to Bryan Street.

We cannot be sure of the identity of the other gentlemen in suits, but it's likely that they would have been managers or overlookers. The young girls at the front were packers while the women in the centre were bakers. Behind them on the right was the all-male maintenance team - the women's lib movement had not even thought about burning their bras and going in for engineering in 1936 - and the boys on the left at the back worked in the tinning shop.

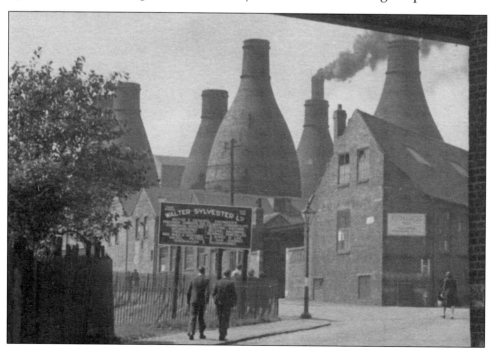

The Warrillow Collection

Left: Iron and steel was manufactured at the Shelton Bar Steelworks for more than 150 years. At one time the works was one of the area's major employers - around the turn of the century Shelton Bar was providing jobs for around 3,000 people. When Lord Granville first leased a large piece of land at Etruria, Hanley and Cobridge in the early 1830s he obviously had an eye for its potential for industry. Everything needed for the development of iron and steel already existed; coal and ironstone mines were already in production nearby, and the neighbouring Trent and Mersey Canal would make bulk transport cheaper. The first blast furnace was operational by 1841, and within twenty years eight furnaces were in production. A forge and a rolling mill were built in the 1850s and Hanley Deep Pit was sunk in 1854. The railway links that were established a few years later became a key part of production - the steelworks' railway terminal sweeps across the foreground of the photograph. The steelworks became a target for World War II bombing raids, and though some damage was done production continued and went on until 1978. This aerial view, bisected by the railway line, gives us some idea of the extent of industry in one area of the Potteries. The huge complex of Shelton Bar Steelworks (which over the years had gradually expanded until it occupied almost five square miles) dominates the background, while the foreground is taken up by Wedgwood's Eritrea works. From the industries' earliest days the high quality coal mined from the nearby colliery formed a key part of both industries - pottery production and ironworking in the area dates back to the 17th Century. Coal mining around the area was causing

subsidence problems as early as the 1840s, when huge cracks were appearing along whole rows of buildings, and houses were collapsing completely as the ground sunk into the rabbit warren of workings below. A view of the area in its heyday must have been like a vision of Dante's Inferno, but today the old heavy industries are almost extinct. Wedgwood's original factory was demolished in 1960 and was replaced by the Evening Sentinel's production plant; Etruria Hall, after functioning for a time as offices, is today a hotel.

Above: This breathtaking rooftop photograph gives us a rare opportunity to view Burslem's famous gilded angel in close up. Manufactured in copper, the figure's full description is as 'a winged figure of Civic Victory descending with the crown and "Meed of Merit"'. The 'Old' Town Hall' was designed after the classical 14th and 15th Italian style by Wolverhampton architect G T Robinson, and William Davenport of Longport Hall laid the foundation stone in May 1854. The building, which cost £10,000, was officially opened on 28th January 1857. The clock tower that presides over the Market Place is supported by ornate stone figures, and when the building was first opened the clock dial was lit by gas. In 1925 the Town Hall clock was replaced and the entire mechanism renewed apart from the bell that sounded the hours. Electricity lit the four new five-foot diameter opal glass dials. Lovers of trivia will enjoy finding out that the clock's pendulum weighs a hundredweight. This was Burslem's third Town Hall, but its use as such was fairly short-lived as the town surrendered its independence in 1911.

The Warrillow Collection

The Warrillow Collection

Above: There was little traffic about on the day this photograph was taken in Wedgwood Place, Burslem, and a few pedestrians and a cyclist add the only movement to the view - apart, of course, from the smoke that drifts skywards from one of the bottle ovens at the Alcock, Lindley and Bloore works.

The part of the works nearest the camera has an interesting history, as the building once formed part of the Burslem Workhouse. Dubbed 'The Bastille' by local people, the workhouse was the dreaded ogre that loomed on the horizon of every family that lived on the edge of poverty. The discipline at the facility was so harsh as to be almost prison-like. The sexes were strictly separated and no contact between husbands and wives was permitted. As if poverty was a crime, the inmates had all their personal possessions confiscated on arrival, when they were given uniforms of cheap and coarse material which they were obliged to wear. They were then locked in and provided with only enough food and sleep to enable them to keep on working - one shilling and threepence-halfpenny was allegedly the sum spent on an inmate's food each week.

Above right: A Red Cross parcel of extra food and provisions was a rare treat in the monotonous lives of prisoners of war, and these St John Ambulance staff pose cheerfully for the camera alongside the Red Cross baskets with the knowledge that theirs was a job well done. These baskets en route to prison camps were sent off from Stoke railway station, and the LMS represen-

tative in the middle (the station master?) checks the paperwork before transportation.

The Red Cross societies were established in all civilised nations under the 1864 Geneva Convention for the care of the wounded in wartime. Those nations signing the Convention agreed that hospitals, ambulances and workers showing the red cross sign should not be fired upon or otherwise molested in their work.

The second world war called for volunteers of both sexes to fulfil all kinds of duties, and everyone pulled their weight. The St John Ambulance workers, the Women's Voluntary Service, the Women's Land Army and the evacuation service all sought recruits. Air Raid Precaution wardens of both sexes were appointed, and men who were outside the age for military service joined the Home Guard.

The method of transportation gives a slightly Eastern feel to this photograph, but the scene was actually captured in Shirleys Bone and Flint Mill in Etruria. It was the potteries' demand for large quantities of ground flint and bone that led to the setting up of the mill in 1857 to supply to the smaller potteries (the larger concerns such as Wedgwood's usually had grinding mills of their own).

The original dry-milling process the flint went through produced a fine dust that proved to be detrimental to the workers' lungs, but the problem was eventually resolved by grinding the flint in water.

The earliest mills were water-powered, which limited the sites available for the building of mills. The Industrial Revolution signalled the arrival of steam power and the beam engine, and after that mills could be built virtually alongside their clients.

Shirley's original canalside mill gradually became run down, though it continued production until 1972 when the introduction of modern machinery led to it being closed abruptly. The firm still trades from modern premises using up-to-date machinery on the same site. The City Museum began to restore the mill in 1978, and the work of volunteers attracted a number of awards.

The Warrillow Collection

The Warrillow Collection

Above: Women have long been extensively employed in the pot banks, from fettling to quality assessment. The better paid workers were the paintresses, whose artistic skills and keen eye for fine detail made them the crème de la crème among the workforce. A marvellous job for creative young women (and one which carried a lot of responsibility), objects receiving that vital finishing touch from the paintresses would perhaps be worth hundreds of pounds. They added their unique touch to a wide range of vases, tableware and other items. This photograph of paintresses in the Wedgwood decorating shop dates from the 1950s. The work

of Daisy Makeig-Jones, who during the 1920s produced the Wedgwood Fairyland series, which depicted brightly coloured elves, pixies and fairies in various dream scenes, is today highly sought-after. A Fairyland lustre pot might today fetch £5,000. As long ago as 1765 Catherine the Great of Russia commissioned an enormous service painted with English landscapes - the service is now in the Hermitage Museum in St Petersburg.

Above right: Buses dominate this nostalgic 1950s scene, though a number of cars shared their stand opposite the Edco earthenware supplies building. The advertising on the rear of the buses really takes us back: Esso petrol, Saxa salt and Rossi's ice cream - they're all there.

Dozens of readers will remember (and could still sing

if pushed) the Esso jingle that rang out from our television sets during the 1950s. Written by David Bernstein at McCann-Erickson, 'The Esso sign means happy motoring' became the longest running jingle that decade. 'Put a tiger in your tank' followed, and the Esso tiger really took off in the 1960s, when countless tiger tails adorned the petrol caps of Britain's cars. Foreign versions followed ('Pack den Tiger in den tank' appeared in Germany). The popular ad gave rise to derivatives such as 'Put a tiger in your tummy' on hamburger stands, while Tiger Beer had it made - they countered with 'Put a Tiger in your tankard'.

Ice cream (though not Rossi's) was among the first products to give birth to a true catch phrase when Walls invented 'Stop me and buy one' in 1923. More than 8,000 salesmen pedalled round our streets with the slogan on their tricycles.

Beauty and versatility for over a century

The firm of Royal Winton has roots in Stoke-on-Trent that go back over one hundred years. Originally known as Grimwade Brothers it was founded by Leonard Lumsden Grimwade in a factory which comprised of a shed and a yard, situated between two rows of cottages. Leonard had shown a natural talent for modelling pottery from an early age and it was in this field that his infant business began.

There was before long a great demand for his work and he was able to ask his older brother, Sidney Richard, another potter, to join him. Early catalogues show that the company produced a wide range of useful domestic items such as toilet sets, wash bowls, soap dishes, bedpans and ceramic hot water bottles. As well as this they manufactured a range of table ware with dinner and teaware being produced in a variety of patterns and shapes.

By 1887, new showrooms were purchased at the Winton Hotel, close to Stoke Station which was convenient for railway visitors who spied the showrooms from the platforms. Records show that profits doubled every year and by 1890, the company was able to open an export department as well as a London showroom.

*Left: Leonard Grimwade, once described as a man 'absolutely alive - restless in activity and audacious in projects'. **Below:** A view of the finishing warehouse taken in 1906.*

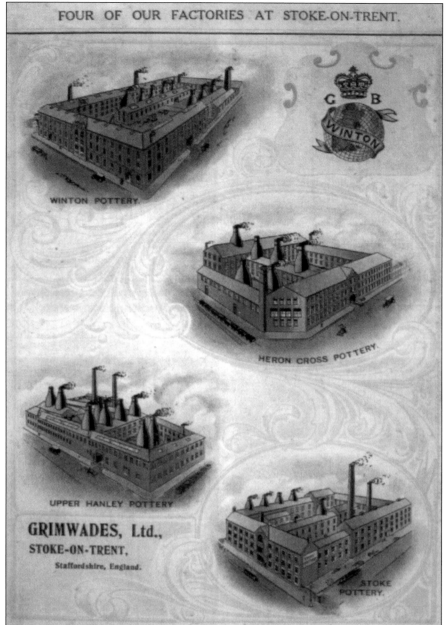

FOUR OF OUR FACTORIES AT STOKE-ON-TRENT.

WINTON POTTERY.

HERON CROSS POTTERY.

UPPER HANLEY POTTERY

GRIMWADES, Ltd.,
STOKE-ON-TRENT,
Staffordshire, England.

STOKE POTTERY.

of Hanley. There followed a decade of expansion and acquisition that the brothers could not have foreseen, although Leonard had once been described as a man 'absolutely alive - restless in activity and audacious in projects'.

Leonard experimented with new methods of manufacture and he developed the Enamel Climax Rotary Kiln, Duplex Lithographic Transfers and other ground breaking techniques.

In 1913 King George V and Queen Mary visited the Potteries and the brothers issued a catalogue to commemorate the event. The royal couple toured the factories before attending an exhibition of the company's products. The queen purchased a Winton Teaset and was delighted to be presented with a gift of a Mecca Foot Warmer (an oval ceramic hot water bottle).

It was at about this time that the first Royal Winton Chintz patterns were launched. These tightly grouped, highly decorative all over floral patterns were to become a milestone in the companies reputation for versatility and beauty. Following an advertisement in the 'Potteries Gazette' in 1929, Royal Winton became the established trade name for Grimwades Ltd, and has remained so through to the present day.

To cope with this expanding trade, the brothers decided to open another factory under the name of Winton Pottery. When finished the total area covered almost two acres and contained some of the most up-to-date equipment available at that time.

It is a measure of the company's success that by 1900, it was able to purchase another factory, the Stoke Pottery. The three potteries (Grimwade Brothers, Winton Pottery and Stoke Pottery) were then amalgamated under the title of Grimwades Limited, with Leonard Grimwade as chairman.

By 1906 more new premises were needed. A new three storey building was opened in October of that year by the Mayor

The First World War had revolutionised industry to such an extent that mass production was the 'only way to go' and Grimwades introduced this method, enjoying the immediate success of being able to despatch orders much more promptly and

Above: Four of the Stoke factories.
Left: One of the re-introduced Royal Winton chintz limited edition pieces.

antique market today.

In 1964 the company was acquired by Howard Pottery Company of Shelton and between that time and today there have been many changes in the company, with several successive owners. Despite this, the name Royal WInton has survived, being synonymous with quality and design.

In 1995 the company was purchased by its current owners who reverted back to the original company name of Grimwades Ltd trading as Royal Winton. They decided to re-introduce some of the more popular Chintz patterns on a range of giftware, tableware and Limited Edition pieces. In March 1997 the first new piece of Royal WInton Chintz for nearlyforty years was introduced and unveiled at the chintz convention in Pasadena, California. A spectacular piece, an 11" octagonal vase in the Florence pattern, it received resounding approval.

The company has witnessed many changes over the past century but one thing has never altered, its dedication to quality and beauty which excites many buyers from all around the world.

increasing output at the same time. By this time, Grimwades employed well over a thousand people.

Above: An early advertisement for the 'Mecca Hot Water Bottle'. Below: The Royal Winton Chintz tea

Leonard Grimwade died in 1931, but his legacy survived and the company went from strength to strength under the leadership of James Plant. Over succeeding decades Royal Winton introduced more than 60 Chintz patterns and became the leading producer of this style of decoration, exporting to most Commonwealth countries and the USA. Discontinued in the 1960s due to the high production costs Royal Winton Chintz has become highly desirable in the

E W Good - quality products for artistic hands

E. W. Good & Co Ltd began life before the First World War and became, in 1918, a formal partnership between brother and sister Ernest Wilberforce Good and Freda Good.

From premises at 30, Barker Street, Longton, which had formerly been a public house called the Union Inn, the new company traded as 'Colour and Size Manufacturers', from the newly named Barker Street Colour Works.

Frits and glazes were also produced in a part of the works that had been used in its public house days as an indoor bowling alley.

'Liquid bright and burnish gold' was advertised and squirrel hair brushes for the application of the golds and colours were imported from France. Sun-bleached natural sponges were imported from the Aegean Island of Kalimnos, the centre of the Greek sponge fishing industry. The sponges were imported in compressed bales before being 'sprung' and sorted in a specially controlled stockroom.

Gas boilers were used for heating and mixing specially imported resins and essential oils. These exotic mixtures, known in the trade as 'fat oils', and 'ground-laying oils', were, and are still, used for mixing with

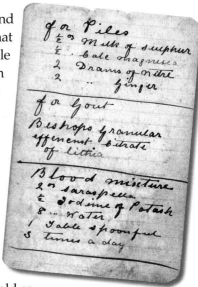

dry ceramic colour and gum turpentine so that ceramic artists are able to paint 'freehand' on glazed ware without the paint drying too quickly. This is known as keeping the paint 'open'. Printing oils were also produced using various grades of both 'raw' and 'boiled' linseed oils. Special 'soft soaps' were prepared and sold as aids to both the highly skilled specialist mouldmakers, and those factories that concentrated on underglaze 'print and enamel' ware.

Other products imported, modified and sold, included gums from the Sudan, turpentine, pine oil and lavender oil from both France and Portugal, together with aniseed, camphor and clove oils from Zanzibar and the Caribbean 'Spice Island' of Grenada.

Above: An early recipe.
Below: Longton before the Clean Air Act.

In 1962 the company had purchased the business of John Harrison, a firm that had traded in Longton as a 'Potters Chemist' as far back as 1875. From this source many traditional recipes that had been closely guarded by 'people in the know' came to E W Good. One in particular being an embrocation recipe for Stoke City Football Club combining 10oz white wine vinegar, 10oz methylated spirits, 10oz turpentine, one part camphor and the white of one egg. Other interesting recipes obtained were cures for 'Piles', 'Gout' and, mysteriously, one for 'Blood Mixture'!

At one stage, shortly after the Second World War, it was decided to use an American-style slogan to boost sales. The company chose "Goods goods are good goods!" This dreadful pun did at least ensure that the firms name was mentioned in four words out of five. The legend currently displayed on the delivery vehicle is 'Goods for the Potteries...' a slogan that is instantly recognised wherever deliveries are being made.

There were no members of the Good family who wished to continue in the business after the retirement of the founders and so it was sold in 1948 to Mr V H Creyke. This well known North Staffordshire gentleman was a particularly keen motorist and regularly visited customers in a highly polished black A C Cobra sports car. This was considered by many to be a very exotic form of transport around the potteries at that time. In due course, Mr Creyke sold the business to a Mr Leslie Shirley, who in the sixties, embarked on a programme of expansion. He formed a partnership with his relation by marriage, Mr Geoffrey Wildblood, whose commercial experience helped when the premises were extended and larger warehouses acquired.

Bulk liquid tanks were installed and a specially designed, fireproof building constructed and licensed by the local authority. This enabled the company to stock and sell a variety of solvents, oils and thinners that were becoming more and more important in the ever-changing decorating shops of the Potteries.

In 1972 the partnership was dissolved and Mr Wildblood took control of the company. It was at this time that he was joined by his son-in-law, Mr Peter Hedley the present Managing Director.

In the UK the company's main markets are the ceramics and glass industries. Fine hair brushes or 'pencils' are supplied to all the top names in the industry including Royal Doulton, Spode, Wedgwood, Royal Worcester, Aynsley, Dudson and the Churchill Group.

Professional artists and illustrators together with film animators, and fine art restoration specialists are also supplied with a range of brushes made both in the UK and imported from France, Germany, Korea and Israel.

Overseas markets include Europe, Scandinavia, Australia, South America, the Far East and the USA.

Solvents, essential oils, paints, traditional mediums and hand made brushes continue to be part of the comprehensive range of products that E W Good offer to the world wide ceramic industry specialising in top quality hand decorated ware.

Top Left: One of the many uses for Good's brushes.
Below: The premises today.

Royal Doulton - The business created by a man of imagination

Royal Doulton of Stoke-on-Trent is the world's largest manufacturer and distributor in the premium ceramic tableware and giftware market. Annual sales are around £250 million, with more than half coming from overseas customers in over eighty countries. Today, Royal Doulton employs around 6,500 people worldwide. It is a thriving organisation, building new markets throughout the world and expanding its range of fine products. It is justifiably proud of its heritage.

The Company was founded in 1815, not in Stoke-on-Trent but in Lambeth, South London, by John Doulton who invested his life savings of £100 and began producing practical stoneware, chiefly bottles and jars, from his small pottery.

John's son, Henry, joined the business in 1835. Described by his biographer, Edmund Gosse, as 'a man of imagination', he was the key figure in the development of the enterprise. Having made his fortune through helping to pioneer modern sanitation by manufacturing stoneware drainpipes, he turned his attention to decorative ware, and was responsible for inaugurating a great period of art pottery wares in the second half of the 19th century. Doulton's Lambeth Studio continued to be a flourishing centre of art pottery until its closure in 1956.

In 1877 Henry Doulton moved to Stoke-on-Trent, purchasing a major shareholding in an old-established pottery, Pinder, Bourne & Company, in Nile Street, Burslem, the 'mother town' of the Potteries. As a newcomer and a Southerner, Henry Doulton was initially regarded with suspicion by the Stoke-on-Trent potters, but gradually he built up the Company's reputation.

At first Henry wished to perfect his production of earthenwares rather than embark on the manufacture of bone china. When he discovered that the factory was developing bone china without his knowledge and marking it 'Doulton' he was so furious that he smashed the samples with his umbrella and left. However, he returned the next day and announced that he had decided to build a bone china factory.

In 1885 Henry was awarded the Society of Arts' Albert Medal, a rare distinction generally reserved for outstanding scientists such as Pasteur and Lord Kelvin. Two years later he was knighted for his services to art and industry and is still regarded as the greatest Victorian potter.

In 1889, Charles Noke joined Doulton at Burslem as a modeller, reviving the tradition of Staffordshire figure manufacture. The first Doulton figures were based on classical and literary themes. Although

Top: John Doulton, founder of the company. *Left: John's son Henry Doulton, who carried on the family business.* *Right: A version of Darling, which was first issued in 1913.*

they were praised by critics, they did not immediately receive popular acclaim. The first one to win public favour was Charles Vyse's simple portrait of a fair-haired boy in a nightdress. When it was shown to Queen Mary during her visit to Burslem in 1913, she exclaimed, 'Isn't he a darling?' So the figure was immediately named 'Darling' in her honour.

With royal approval, demand for Royal Doulton figures grew. In a Company brochure from the mid nineteen thirties the Royal Doulton figure Princess Badoura is listed at £120. In 1998 this was the most expensive figure in the Royal Doulton range, selling for £13,250.

The high quality of Doulton's wares had received recognition from Edward VII, who in 1901 granted permission for the company to prefix

Top right: Queen Mary pictured during her visit to the Nile Street Factory in 1913. **Right:** *A view of Royal Doulton's decorating workshop in 1910.* **Below:** *Workers outside the Royal Doulton Factory in Nile Street, Burslem at the turn of the century.*

its name with 'Royal' and awarded it the Royal Warrant. In 1966 the company again won royal acclaim when it was awarded the Queen's Award for Technological Achievement for its development of an entirely new ceramic body. It was the first china manufacturer to be honoured with this award.

During the sixties and seventies Royal Doulton made a number of acquisitions, including Minton.

Thomas Minton, a master engraver by trade founded a pottery in Stoke under his own name in 1793. Early production centred on underglaze blue printed tablewares and in c1798 bone china was introduced, with great success. In 1836 Thomas's son Herbert took control and began producing inlaid floor and decorative wall tiles, Parian figures and Majolica glazes securing for Minton the Bronze Medal at the Great Exhibition of 1851.

Colin Minton Campbell inherited his uncle Herbert's factory in 1858 and introduced pate-sur-pate, the three dimensional form of decoration, and, was the first to acquire the Patent Rights for the Acid Gold Process in 1863 which provided a bas-relief gold finish. Gold remains a Minton speciality. Today, a single Minton plate represents up to three weeks' work by a skilled raised paste gold artist, and hence can cost several thousand pounds.

'Haddon Hall' is Minton's best selling tableware pattern and is especially popular in Japan.

*Top: The Minton China Factory, London Road, pictured from the Minton Earthenware Works in 1945. **Left:** Thomas Minton, founder of the Minton Factory.*

The International Headquarters of Royal Doulton in London Road, Stoke was formerly the Minton factory.

In 1969 the Royal Doulton Company bought John Beswick which had been established since 1894. The first Beswick, James, had been a potter of the 'old school'. His son and partner John gained some technical training from attending classes at the Pottery School in Tunstall. John's son John Ewart, had no successor, hence the sale to Doulton. At the end of the sixties, in addition to animal, bird and figure ranges, there were over 100 different ornamental items in production alongside tableware. By the end of 1973, however, all tableware and vase production had ceased.

Top: Charles Noke, Royal Doulton's Art Director, surrounded by examples of the company's range of figure and animal models. He is pictured in 1932, four years before his retirement. Left: Paintresses in their 'pinnies' working on Royal Doulton Character and relief-moulded jugs, 1947.

Left: HM The Queen, then Princess Elizabeth visited the factory in 1949 and admired the skills of Mrs Thurza Fulford and Mrs Myra Lewis, cup handlers at the Nile Street Factory for more than forty years.
Below left: A recording being made at the Minton Factory, Stoke, of the radio programme 'Down Your Way' in 1951.
Bottom right: Eyes meeting across the ware boards at Royal Doulton's Burslem Factory during the late 1940s.

and floral decorations. Its products are sold throughout the world and its 'Old Country Roses' design is one of the most popular bone china patterns of all time, having sold over 100 million pieces since its introduction in 1962.

Since 1993 Royal Doulton has been an independent listed company. The Royal Doulton Factory in Nile Street, Burslem is the site of the Royal Doulton Visitor Centre where members of the public can tour the factory and see in the museum the world's largest public collection of Royal Doulton figures.

Among products currently manufactured at the John Beswick Studios in Longton are Royal Doulton's Character Jugs and figures from Royal Doulton's famous 'Bunnykins' nurseryware collection; both ranges were first introduced by Charles Noke in 1934.

In 1972 Royal Doulton was bought by Pearson, and this merger with Allied English Potteries brought a number of key brands, noted for their excellence and heritage, into the Royal Doulton family. Of these Royal Crown Derby, based in Derby, was the oldest china brand; its first known piece is dated 1750 and it was granted permission by George III to incorporate the crown in the backstamp on all its wares. Many early Crown Derby designs and shapes are still in production today, notably the distinctive 'Imari' design which was developed in the mid 19th century for tableware and later extended to giftware. It is currently used on a wide variety of popular collectables such as paper-weights.

Royal Albert became part of Royal Doulton in 1972. The success of Royal Albert lies in its essentially English style with delicate flutes, flowing curves

Top left: Young paintresses in the Enamel Department at Beswick's Gold Street Works in Longton decorate the popular 'Palm Tree' series, Christmas 1950. **Above right:** Royal Albert's 'Old Country Roses', introduced in 1962.
Below: The Royal Doulton Factory in Nile Street, Burslem today.

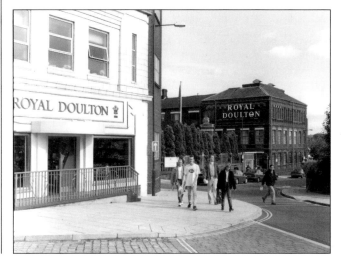

The Dudson Group - Setting tables and standards

Richard Dudson, father of the renowned Dudson Group, was born near Stoke in 1768. Like many of his local contemporaries, he quickly mastered the potter's art and established the company in Hope Street, Hanley in 1800. Whilst many neighbouring potteries faced bankruptcy, Richard prospered and quickly earned a reputation for decorative, yet useful items. When his two sons, and later his grandson, James, assumed control of the business they developed a distinctive line of beautifully decorated jasper ware. The business thrived, attracting orders and commissions from all over the country for its fine figures, as well as satisfying a robust Victorian appetite for more utilitarian, affordable items which Dudsons fashioned on a

particularly durable range of stoneware bodies that James himself had developed.

James' son, James Thomas, took over the business in 1880, and it was he who masterminded the most significant turning point in the company's history. In his extensive travels, generating business, he discerned a swelling tide of demand from the hotel and restaurant trade. The nineteenth century taste for travel, spawned by the railway mania of the 1840s and nurtured by a popular fascination with the growth of the Empire, saw unprecedented numbers of people spending time away from home, and the birth of the 'Grand Hotel'. The catering industry was in the ascendant and James shrewdly anticipated the merits of specialising for this market. By 1891, the Hope Street factory had ceased to produce domestic ware and was exclusively committed to catering lines - a narrower range of items, but in greatly increased quantities.

When, in 1899, James Thomas was succeeded by his two sons, James Robert and Harry, the company was supremely positioned for the dawn of the new century, and its stoneware and, most notably, Jasper ware (in 'A Descriptive Account of the Potteries' 1893) 'as well known and highly esteemed as any product of its class'. More than a decade of successful consolidation followed until Harry's untimely death from TB in 1913 and the outbreak of the First World War. James Robert's own sons, Roy and Rex, had entered the firm but were instantly called up. Dudsons faced a bleak time: no Dudson at the helm, and export markets to USA, Canada, the Continent and India severely disrupted. Henry Bagnall was appointed works manager, and it is a testament to his loyalty and to the dedication of the workforce, not to mention the stalwart devotion of the Dudson wives and sisters, that the firm survived the war at all. But survive it did, returning to the control of Rex and Hubert (his younger brother) in 1918 and gaining limited company status in the same year.

Trade was buoyant - the post-war explosion in the travel and hotel industries yielded rich rewards and Dudson customers now included shipping lines - such as Pacific Steam Navigation and Royal Mail - grand hotels across the globe and a plethora of railway companies. Hubert's decision in the 1930s to expand the wholesaling side of the business meant an improved service for all clients and saw Dudson's as factors for many Ridgway lines and even some glass and cutlery.

The Second World War brought its own challenges, including the Limitation of Supply Act which

Top: Richard Dudson's business card. **Left:** *James Thomas Dudson, great grandson of the founder.*

The Hope Street factory eventually closed in 1980, and all production moved to Burslem and Tunstall, but its Grade II listed bottle oven has had a new lease of life as a major tourist attraction at the heart of a lottery-funded scheme to convert the Hope Street site into a resource for local voluntary groups. And a museum there will be devoted to the 200 year history of a remarkable family firm - the oldest private business of its type, spanning nine generations and still going from strength to vitrified strength - the Dudson Group.

restricted output. But Hubert was already planning for post-war development.

In 1947 Hubert's son, Derek, joined the business at the start of a dynamic era of expansion. First came the acquisition of the Albert Potteries in Burslem and then the purchase of the Grindley Hotelware Co. Ltd in Tunstall. Trading links were established in Canada and Australia, but by the 1960s it was product development that marked Dudson out at the head of the field. The firm was instrumental in establishing the rigorous British Standard 4034 for Vitrified Hotel Ware. And then in 1983 after five years' intensive research, came the triumphant appearance of the remarkable Dudson Fine China 'body', a major breakthrough in ceramic technology that combines the strength of super vitrified ware with the delicate beauty of bone china.

Above: The rear of the Hope Street Factory at Hanley where the business began. The company moved from these premises in 1980. *Below:* Some of the attractive jugs produced by the company.

Aynsley - *a name synonymous with fine china*

Aynsley is one of the best known and most respected names in the Staffordshire Potteries tracing its origins back to the eighteenth century. At that time John Aynsley I came to Lane End, part of the present day Longton, attracted by the new and developing industries of pottery and mining. He soon proved himself an able and enterprising entrepreneur, establishing a workshop producing a wide range of wares, best known by collectors today for the coloured transfer-printed decoration on the then fashionable cream and pearlwares, the engraving signed 'John Aynsley Lane End'. For a time he was part-owner with Josiah Spode and other Staffordshire potters of the Fenton Park Colliery Company, a local mining venture. He died in 1829, a noted figure credited with introducing lustre to that part of the Potteries.

The most famous member of the family is probably his grandson whose career spans the remainder of the century. Involved in the potting trade from a young age and finishing his apprenticeship with the well known firm of Minton in Stoke, the young John Aynsley II was, through shrewdness, enterprise and application, able to build in 1861 a large and imposing new factory

which he called the Portland Works. The building which is still today the home of Aynsley China has an imposing front facade with classical features and Venetian window which was no doubt intended by the proprietor to reflect the high quality bone china produced within. Certainly John Aynsley designed the interior to give light and well-ventilated conditions for his workers, showing a concern for their welfare which was all too rare at that date.

From this time Aynsley became best known for its fine bone china, specialising in breakfast, tea and dessert wares. In particular the company sold many of its productions in the United States and Canada, with John Aynsley himself visiting New York in 1880. Artists were engaged to hand decorate dessert services which were then richly gilded, local Canadian views appealing to buyers in that market.

Above: John Aynsley II, "The grand old man of Longton", during his time as Mayor of Longton, 1886-1890. Left: The Portland Works, built by John Aynsley II and pictured on the occasion of a Royal Visit.

As a leading Longton china manufacturer, John Aynsley took especial pride in his community. His tremendous energies were employed to the full as mayor, serving four terms of office from 1886 to 1890. He was responsible for the Queen's Park, the first public park in the Potteries, as well as contributing both money and time to the Longton hospital, one of his many charitable causes. He was famous for handing out money to the needy and he established a fund for the old people of the area to distribute a little cheer at Christmas time. Truly he had become "the grand old man of Longton".

Prince Charles. At the present time Michael Aynsley, the seventh generation member of the founder of the Portland Works, is equally involved in its future success, now as the member of a group which also embraces the famous names of Belleek China and Galway Crystal.

Above: A very early utility vehicle.
Left: A John Aynsley of Lane End Jug, made at the time of the French Revolution and entitled 'French Happiness', depicting starving and poorly clothed Frenchmen. 'English Misery', pictured on the reverse depicts well-clothed Englishmen eating roast beef and plum pudding. The teapot is transfer printed and dates from 1800.

Below: Two loving cups made by John Aynsley II - one made for his grandson in 1888, the other to commemorate his eightieth birthday on December 11th 1903.

After his death in 1907, he was succeeded by his son and grandson as one generation followed another. Many times in the present century the firm has received royal patronage and support. Prince Edward the Prince of Wales visited the Portland Works in 1924, to be followed by his brother, later King George VI, in 1931. The present Queen, at the time of her wedding in 1947, selected an Aynsley service as her gift from the British Pottery Manufacturers' Federation, a tradition which was continued when Princess Diana also chose an Aynsley rose patterned service when she married

Supplying the needs of local customers

It was way back in 1899 when Enoch James opened his tripe factory and chip shop in Pinnox Street, Tunstall, along with his three brothers who were also involved in the business.

Before long Enoch's son E G James (Bert) began to trade in meat and pies, which were made by Mrs Rigby, and the two businesses ran in tandem.

Enoch's son, E G James, got into the Army during the First World War, by lying about his age, as did many patriotic young men at the time. When he was demobbed he, together with a partner, set up the Model Meat Factory in Hanley in 1927.

In 1934 E G James bought a motor bike

Top left: Enoch Gimbert James outside the Macclesfield Street Shop, circa 1926.
Right: Standing from left, Harry Heath, Joe Miles and Graham Walters, Alec James with Clifford James kneeling.

with a sidecar for making deliveries which was ridden by employee Stan Phillips. When war broke out again in 1939 a shortage of petrol forced him to revert to butchers' carrier bikes. When supplies improved, the firm acquired three blue Austin vans, well remembered by some people for the plates of sausages painted on the sides.

In 1938 Harry Heath (who later married Berts daughter) joined the business, and when Enoch the founder retired, Albert Clowes (who started as an apprentice with Enoch in 1938) a skilled producer of tripe, joined E G James, so that the firm once more was involved with the tripe trade, and also produced cooked pies and sausages in the factory.

umbrella in 1996.

Ethel and Harry Heath had two daughters, Jane and Mary. These two ladies are now the mainstay of the business. Jane's husband, Leon Bagguley is the present production manager. Officially, Jane Bagguley is

There was a shortage of male staff during the war and displaced persons and refugees helped to fill the gaps and keep the business fully manned. Ethel James, E G's daughter, had been working in Grindley's pottery factory but she had to give this up during the war so that she could run the office for her father. His two sons, Clifford and Alec, also came into the business.

All through the period from 1937 to the present day the company ran a market stall in Tunstall. In 1955 E G James became a limited company, Albert Clowes helped the firm set up a tripe factory in Ford Green in the late fifties and in 1956 a butcher's shop was opened in Town Road, Hanley which remained open until 1974.

When E G James retired in 1964 his sons and daughter carried on the various enterprises between them. Alec James took charge of the tripe business, Clifford was responsible for the shops in Hanley and Macclesfield Street and daughter Ethel and husband Harry took over the factory and market stall. When Clifford James retired, the Macclesfield Street shop was leased to butchers outside the family until Ethel's daughters brought it back under the family

shop manager and her sister Mary Jones is in charge of the market and office but neither of them is too proud and the two ladies find themselves filling most roles in the business when occasion demands.

The company has seen many changes since the founding of the tripe business at the turn of the century. Many of its well-loved traditional recipes are the same but in every other way E G James Limited has kept pace with the times. Current legislation on Health and Safety and Food Hygiene has always been strictly observed and the company has invested in the latest refrigeration technology as it has become available.

Top left: The tripe factory premises pictured in the late 1950s. Below: The shop on Macclesfield Street in June 1986.

The story of the Potato King

On May 25th 1896 Arthur Roberts married Rosa Worthington at St James' Church in the parish of Longton.

They ran their green-grocer shop at 105/107 Sutherland Road, Longton. Arthur's father Herbert was also a greengrocer. In 1901 Arthur took stall number 11 in Borough Market, Market Lane which is now known as Longton Market. He began with a barrow to push and progressed to a horse and cart.

The couple's first son, another Arthur, had sadly died in infancy. Their next son James was born in 1900. Sons Harry and another Arthur followed, as did three daughters, Esther May, Ethel and Rosa. All members of the family were recruited as soon as they were able to wield a brush or lift a bag of carrots. The ladies did most of the office work. As the founder could neither read nor write he had to allow them to do the books.

There was a move to Market Lane, Longton, in the 1920s. The premises here were gas lit and at one end of the warehouse candles were used.

The two elder sons went into the family business which by now had become a wholesale concern as well as running two retail businesses. The yard at Sutherland Road was given over to it and part of the premises became a banana room.

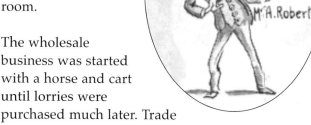

The wholesale business was started with a horse and cart until lorries were purchased much later. Trade thrived and a warehouse was acquired in Transport

Top left: Mr Arthur Roberts, founder of the company. Above: A charming caricature of Mr Roberts. Below: A very early delivery vehicle, a Model T Ford being driven by James Roberts, Arthur can be seen in the shop doorway with his daughter Rosa.

Lane. By this time the youngest son Arthur was also involved in the business. The firm stayed here until the development of Longton in the sixties. After the compulsory purchase of the old premises to make way for the Longton precinct the business moved to St Martin's Lane.

Arthur senior continued to travel to Manchester to do all the buying whilst the sons did all the delivering to the local shops. The stock was loaded on to carriages pulled by horses. A porter would take the goods to the station where they were loaded into a wagon which was attached to a passenger train. There were no chilled articulated lorries in those days!

James' son, yet another Arthur (known as young Arthur) and Harry's son, also Harry came into the business on leaving school. War broke out in 1939 and its main effect on the greengrocery trade was a shortage of bananas. Deliveries were hampered by petrol rationing.

Arthur senior died in December 1948. He had been a well known figure in Longton who was never seen without his bowler hat. Known throughout the trade as the Potato King, his

Above: Arthur and Rosa Roberts with their three children outside their grocery shop on Sutherland Road.

favourite pastime was bowls. He was a member of the Dunrobin Bowling club, founded in 1898 and he was also a Mason.

The business continued under the two older brothers, James and Harry with younger brother, Arthur's help. Headquarters was the premises in St Martin's Lane with the original site in Sutherland Road still being used for packing. Harry junior's eldest son Michael entered the business in 1968, followed by younger brother Mark some eight years later. In 1973 James too died and by the early eighties brother Arthur had retired.

When Harry senior died in 1982 the business continued with Harry and James' son Arthur, at the helm. In 1983 the company took over the business and premises of James Preece. Now part of the Albert Fisher Group in George Court, Longton, the business was still being conducted from St Martin's Lane.

During the late eighties new premises were built in George Court from where the company now operates. At this time more and more produce was being procured directly from farms in this country, or directly imported from Holland and France.

The company returned once again to the retail business with the opening of fruit shops in Meir and Stone,

Above: Arthur Roberts and Sons ration card giving the company authority to purchase potatoes.
Below: Michael and Mark at George Court.

and later, with concessions within a well-known supermarket, in Longton, Hanley, Crewe and Nantwich.

By this time, after the retirement of young Arthur and Harry Junior, the business was being run by Harry junior's two sons, Michael and Mark, the fourth generation of management who oversaw some 53 staff.

The business was very much a male organisation until the late seventies. The office manager Ernest Sherwin, a long serving employee, then engaged a female to help run the office. On Mr Sherwin's retirement in the early eighties, Harry junior's daughter Mandy joined the company as accounts clerk. The office is run today by Mark's wife, Kath, that very first female employee. Mandy now works on the retail side of the business.

The one permanent resident at St Martin's Lane was the warehouse cat who was often seen prowling around. One day a customer who owned a wet fish and greengrocers shop inadvertently left the tailgate of his car open whilst collecting some produce. When a loud shout was heard, everyone looked up to see the said cat leaping out of the back of the car with a large and succulent plaice hanging from her mouth. The customer could soon be seen half way down the road in hot pursuit of the cat and his property. Knowing it would be in disgrace, the cat kept a very low profile for the rest of the day and the customer was a lot more careful in future.

Another animal that made its mark was a horse who would often turn up back in the yard in Sutherland Road, still complete with its load of goods. When he considered he had been kept waiting too long outside a shop he would take it upon himself to make his own way home.

"THE HORSE WOULD OFTEN TURN UP BACK IN THE YARD AT SUTHERLAND ROAD, STILL COMPLETE WITH ITS LOAD OF GOODS!"

Above: A view of the very well stocked warehouse in St. Martins Lane.

At Hanley's heart - a shopping heaven

Step into the Potteries Shopping Centre in Hanley and you're in a different world: a world of light and air, marble and mirrors, where the arching stems of lush vegetation welcome you to a haven of shopping.

Ninety six stores, on three levels, open their doors here daily - including all the favourite High Street names: from Timpson to Tie Rack, Dolcis to Debenhams, and incorporating Littlewoods. But that's not all - over 120 traditional stalls operate in the Market Hall, baby changing facilities, a Food Court with cafés and fast food outlets for hungry visitors, even a playcentre where young children can be entertained in safety while Mum tackles the all-important weekly shop, or steals a couple of precious hours to browse in peace for that special outfit or all-important gift.

This dramatic new retail Centre stands in the pedestrianised centre of modern Hanley, between Market Square, Town Road and across Quadrant Road. Formerly used as an open-air car park, the site had long been earmarked by the City for a shopping development. Hanley, served as it is by excellent road and rail links, stands at the centre of a wide catchment area that includes Manchester, Derby, Wolverhampton and Birmingham. Altogether, 750,000 shoppers live within a mere 30

minutes' drive. The site cried out for a big scheme and Capital Shopping Centres plc (managing agents for Capital and Counties) were quick to see its potential. Their expertise in developing and managing retail centres in locations as diverse as Newcastle, Bromley and Watford equipped them perfectly for a Midlands challenge, and they took it up with enthusiasm.

Work on the Centre began in September 1985 and took three years to complete, at a cost of £45 million. Even before the official opening, it was clear that the Potteries Centre was going to have a vital impact on the area - not just because of its stunning architecture (designed by Michael Haskoll Associates of London) but also for the dramatic contribution it would make to the local economy. Employment opportunities sprang up immediately with construction work, and subsequently a plethora of jobs became available as the Potteries' shops and

Above: The impressive entrance to the Potteries Shopping Centre. **Left:** *The Entrance Mall.*

splendid view of the Centre's beautiful interior. The Food Court upstairs has seating for over 400 people in an ambience that feels, with its bright light and myriad plants, almost al fresco - though of course it's pleasantly warm and dry all year round, whatever the weather outside!

High up on the Roof Level are Baby Changing Facilities, the Playcentre and another café. Facilities abound throughout the Centre and not just for the able-bodied - a shopmobility service ensures that a manual or electric wheelchair, or an electric scooter, can be borrowed entirely free of charge, complete with a voluntary escort if desired.

The Potteries Centre is genuinely a place for everyone to relish and enjoy, offering as it does a harmony of the most modern facilities with the timeless importance of that old value - the care of the customer. The Potteries Shopping Centre is without doubt one of the most popular and well cared-for centres throughout the country.

stores swung into action on 1 June 1988. Over 1000 people now work at the Centre, not to mention nearly 50 who are employed directly by the Potteries Centre Management.

For the visitor, the result is a shopping experience which is both up-to-the-minute and deeply satisfying. Whether you arrive by car (there's an on-site car park for 1200 cars with its own link bridge into the centre) or by foot, the visual impact is magnificent. Arriving from the main entrance on Market Square, the shopper is greeted by a floor mosaic which incorporates the soft pinks and blues of the Potteries Centre logo. Passing along the marble-pillared Entrance Mall, the Centre soon opens impressively out to reveal a dramatic view of the different levels. Plants, even trees, abound - thriving in the natural light provided by the glazed roofs above. Mirrors enhance the atmosphere of light and space, whilst marble surfaces lend a pristine beauty to the Centre's open areas.

Access to the Lower Mall and Market Hall, or to the Upper Mall above is easy: either by escalator or, more dramatically, by one of the glass wall climber lifts which speed silently upwards to allow another

Above: The West Atrium. ***Below:*** *The Food Court.*

The company with an eye for opportunity

Lycetts Burslem Ltd was founded in 1885 by Charles Lycett, its premises being an old pottery building. This had formerly belonged to Enoch Woods in Pack Horse Lane, Burslem. Mr Lycett rented the top room from Henry Steele, estate agents and started the manufacture of wooden venetian blinds and inside roller blinds.

Being a keen sportsman and cyclist, he branched out in the retail cycle business in rooms below his original one. This did well and later his son Frank Lycett extended the business with motorcycles.

With the advent of war in 1939 and the decline of the motor cycle industry, it was decided to concentrate once more on the blind business with the emphasis on war-time blackout blinds. Under the direction of Ernest Lycett, Frank's son, the manufacture of wood, and later steel, roller shutters was started in 1947.

The business expanded and it was evident that larger premises were required. In 1957 the firm moved to Mars Street, Smallthorne. Then, the next year Mr Michael Lycett,

Top: Charles and Frank Lycett pictured after winning a 20 mile road race in 1906. *Above: Motor cycle business flourished during the 1920s & 30s.* *Left: An early advertisement for Lycetts.*

Ernest's son, joined the company after a period of employment with British Aluminium Company and National Service in the Royal Signals.

Further expansion led to another move. Premises were taken in Glendale Street, Burslem, the company's present address. Here there was ample room for parking and future extension.

Mr Robert Lycett joined the company in 1968 to develop the blinds and awnings business. The company is currently owned equally by Michael and Robert Lycett.

Since returning to Burslem, the company has continued to expand and, in 1979, the window blind section was separated into a wholly owned subsidiary under Lycett Bros (Blinds & Awnings)

Ltd, manufacturing all types of interior blinds - roller, venetian and vertical louvre - as well as manually and electrically controlled exterior awnings, including the increasingly popular 'wet-look' range of materials. This became the responsibility of Mr Robert Lycett.

Lycetts is also the only firm in North Staffordshire to manufacture a complete range of doors. Its wide range includes sectional overhead doors, security

grilles and fire doors to name but a few. Lycetts' fire doors are designed to withstand fire for at least four hours. Another specialisation is entrances to factory premises, including doorways big enough to cope with a double decker bus.

Trade expanded in Britain as architects realised the importance of dealing with one manufacturer for all their industrial door needs. Now the company's name is becoming renowned throughout the far and middle East.

The company continued to expand and trade successfully and, in 1978, admitted the first non-family member to the management team. He was Geoff Clarke who was recruited from a local

engineering company and appointed Works Manager.

In 1987 Michael Lycett took over the running of the company and supervised the accreditation to BS 5750. Certified fire shutters were added to the product range, helping to ensure the company's continued progress.

Geoff Clarke left Lycett in 1990 to set up his own business. He was replaced by Paul Hewson, an experienced engineer who served until 1994.

The company treats its workforce well and is rewarded by long and loyal service. The record must be held by William Mitchell who served the company for 75 years, finally retiring in 1982

Top: Mr Michael Lycett (centre) with site engineers Fred Laughton and Albert Burton in 1960. Above: An early delivery vehicle. Right: Mr Michael Lycett with local distributor Fahad Aldrees at Saudi Build, Riyadh 1996.

Designed to please

1960. Their pieces were now backstamped 'Portmeirion Ware Gray's Pottery England'. As orders increased, manufacturing problems became more serious. In order to have something to sell they began to stock imported Swedish Glass, and Scandinavian glass remained a popular part of the Portmeirion range for many years.

The next major step forward was in 1961 when Susan and Euan acquired the run-down Kirkham's Pottery; after major renovation the Grays business was moved into the new premises. The company was renamed Portmeirion Potteries Ltd and the backstamps now read 'Portmeirion Designed by Susan Williams-Ellis Made In England'.

Portmeirion Pottery came into being on 1 January 1960. The company had previously been known as Gray's Potteries, which may well be remembered for its association with Susie Cooper in the 1920s. Its association with Portmeirion dates back to before the Second World War. Mr A E Gray was a long-standing friend of Sir Clough Williams-Ellis, the designer of the famous italiante village in North Wales, Portmeirion, and had produced tableware banded in Sir Clough's favourite colours for the hotel. When Susan Williams-Ellis, Clough's daughter, wanted an exclusive range of souvenirs for the shop which she and her husband Euan Cooper-Willis managed at the holiday village, Gray's Potteries used Susan's designs to decorate a variety of pottery pieces. The first design, featuring a lady in Welsh costume, was followed by others, all produced exclusively for Portmeirion and bearing the Gray's Potteries yellow ship backstamp.

In 1957 Susan and Euan opened a second Portmeirion shop in London's Pont Street. Increased demand gave rise to problems as Mr Gray had retired and the business was in decline. The solution seemed to be for Susan and Euan to buy the business, and this they did on 1 January

Since then Portmeirion has seen tremendous growth, producing a long succession of Susan's brilliant designs and expanding its export markets, particularly in the USA, Canada, Australia and New Zealand. In 1986, the same year that the new three-storey extension to the the factory at Kirkham Street-London Road was completed, Portmeirion USA was established as a joint venture, and the company's international success received official recognition in 1990 when Portmeirion Potteries (Holdings) PLC received the Queen's Award for Export - a tremendous tribute to Susan Williams-Ellis' energy, determination and above all her design brilliance.

Top Left: Susan Williams-Ellis, founder of Portmeirion Potteries Ltd. Centre: Her father's village, Portmeirion in Wales. Right: Just a small sample from the wide range of Portmeirion ware.

Toffee like Grandfather made...

Walkers' Nonsuch is one of England's finest and oldest makers of traditional toffee. Based in Longton, Stoke on Trent, the family owned and run company has been making toffee to traditional family recipes since the turn of the Century.

Established for more than 100 years Walkers' remains at the forefront of the toffee market, supplying its world famous toffee to customers in more than 25 countries around the globe.

Toffee production is now managed by Ian Walker, grandson of the company founder, Edward Joseph Walker, and the third generation of the Walker family to manage the company since business first started in the late 1800's.

The traditional family recipe has changed very little over the past 100 years. Walkers' still insists on using only the finest natural ingredients in its toffee - raw cane brown sugar, glucose, full cream condensed milk, vegetable oil and butter - many of which are sourced from exotic destinations around the world.

Walkers' has come a long way since the business was established at the turn of the Century. Former potter, Edward Joseph Walker, opened a small sweet shop in Longton, along with his sister, Florence, who helped out in the shop and managed the books for him.

Much to the delight of his local customers Edward began to sell a selection of toffee made in the back of the shop to his own recipes. Demand for Edward's homemade toffee grew so rapidly that he was forced to open a small factory in the old King Street area of Longton to cope with production.
In 1915 Edward enrolled his son, Edward Victor, to help with production. Together they manufactured their toffee, one batch at a time, to Edward Joseph's original recipe. Thus Walkers' Nonsuch was born, later established as an independent company with limited liability in 1922.

Walkers' Nonsuch takes its name from Henry VIII's legendary 'Nonsuch' palace. Crowned the 'palace of all palaces' for its exquisite splendor there was 'nonsuch' like it. This was similar to Edward's reputation as the creator of the most delicious toffee 'nonsuch' like any other.

Business flourished and Edward's toffee continued to be enjoyed by an ever increasing number of customers. However, with the onset of the Second World War and in the post war years Walkers' was forced to restrict its output, finding it increasingly difficult to source its raw materials.

After the war, when restrictions were lifted and business began to

Top right: The old shop where Edward Joseph Walker began making his toffee. Top left: Edward Joseph Walker, founder of the company. Left: An early delivery vehicle.

Increasing production in the seventies made it possible for Walkers' to seriously consider the supply of overseas markets. The company therefore began an active search for agents, visiting export sales outlets and discussing listings with the possibility of exporting the toffee overseas.

The export market remains a key area of business for Walkers' today with customers in many different countries enjoying the pure taste of Walkers' Nonsuch toffee.

While Walkers' recipes have changed very little since the 1800s, great advances have been made in technology and packaging. A continual programme of reinvestment in the business has resulted in machinery and equipment specifically designed to perfect the traditional toffee making process.

The pre-mixed ingredients are distributed around the factory to continuous cookers and then deposited into moulds ready for finishing, Every half hour samples are tested to maintain the correct balance of ingredients in the mix. Walkers' decision to invest in specialist equipment has resulted in an increase in efficiency and speed of production whilst ensuring the consistency and quality of the finished product.

grow again Walkers' decided to move to larger premises. The new site on Calverley Street, Longton had been a sweet factory since it was built in 1894, previously belonging to boiled sweet manufacturer, Horleston Brothers Ltd. Calverley Street is still the home to Walkers' today, following the acquisition of Horleston Brothers in 1947 and Siddalls Blue Churn Confectionery later in 1961.

On the death of Edward Victor Walker in 1962 Ian Walker and his late brother Edward were appointed joint managing directors of the family firm. The brothers set about investing in modern equipment enabling them to produce Walkers' toffees by the ton. Ian and Edward watched over the production at every stage to ensure that the toffee remained of the excellent standard set by their father and grandfather before them.

In addition to these technological advances Walkers' has responded to changing consumer needs and market demands. The traditional method of packing toffee in trays has been updated with the development of Walker' 'crack packs'. Toffee is now moulded into bars and individually wrapped in clear cellophane.

Firmly established in the midlands, the popularity of Walkers' toffee soon spread to the whole of the United Kingdom. During the fifties the company began to receive enquiries from export buyers, interested in purchasing Walkers' toffee for sale overseas.

Top left: A selection of Walkers' Nonsuch toffees. Right: An aerial view of the Calverley Street premises.

Secretary in 1997, and the present co-directors, Lawrence Brown and Adrian Hill.

The present generation of the Walker family intends to continue the traditions lovingly begun by Edward Joseph Walker more than 100 years ago. As the millennium approaches and the industry develops further, Walkers' will continue to produce its delicious toffee, 'Nonsuch' like any other, which is a pleasure to give and receive.

Each bar is pre-segmented making it easier to eat - just tap once while still in its wrapper and the toffee breaks into easy to eat segments. The packets are then supplied to retailers on the old fashioned metal toffee trays that once contained slab toffee for retailers to break up on demand.

During the eighties the company did wonder if the toffee they were producing was an aphrodisiac! One quarter of the female employees became pregnant at the same time and the company was featured on the BBC's 'That's Life' programme with Ester Rantzen plying ladies in London with Walkers' Nonsuch toffee to see if it 'put them in the mood'.

Walkers' Nonsuch continues to be a family concern with Ian's daughters, Kate and Emma involved in sales and nephew Edward Nicholas Walker responsible for production. Traditional family values remain evident in the Walkers' philosophy and its reputation for quality toffee remains unchallenged.

Over the years there have been many loyal employees working with Ian's Grandfather, Father and himself. Particularly Cyril Jackson, who completed 50 years of service as Company

Top left: Showing HRH The Duke of Kent around a display of Walker Nonsuch's products in 1983.
Left: A letter from HRH The Queen Mother thanking the company for her birthday present in 1994. ***Above right:*** Lawrence Brown with past employee, Elsie Frost. ***Below:*** Keeping it in the family - Ian Walker, standing left and his nephew Edward with Ian's daughters Katie and Emma.

CLARENCE HOUSE
S.W.1

2nd August 1994

Dear Mr Walker,

Your kind message to Queen Elizabeth The Queen Mother has been received with much pleasure, as has the gift you have sent to Her Majesty.

The Queen Mother has asked me to write to thank you and all at Walkers' Nonsuch Limited for these birthday wishes, which add so much to the happiness of the occasion.

I am to say how much Her Majesty appreciated the little hammer which was enclosed with your delicious toffee. It was a most thoughtful touch.

Yours sincerely,

Lady-in-Waiting

I. M. Walker, Esq.,
Managing Director.

The College whose students are too enthusiastic

On Friday 10 April 1970 Mr Harold Wilson, Prime Minister, had a very special engagement in his diary . . . the official opening of the City of Stoke-on-Trent Sixth Form College.

Harold Wilson's government had made many changes to the education system, one of the fundamental changes being the abolition of the 11-plus exam. This was an examination which all pupils sat at the age of eleven, and their performance in this examination could have an impact on their whole future careers as places at grammar school were offered to those pupils who scored the highest marks. Many people felt that system was very unjust, and indeed Stoke-on-Trent had made a resolution, as far back as 1955, to renounce the 11-plus examination. In 1955 this proposal was looked on as revolutionary, but with the advent of the Labour government it became reality. Stoke-on-Trent continued to be at the forefront of educational reform; Robert Cant, Chairman of the Education Committee and Alderman Harold Naylor, the Chief Education Officer of Stoke-on-Trent, were involved in the compilation of a report on a visit to the United States of America in April-June 1963 entitled "American Journey - A study of American High Schools". This study was very influential in the creation of the educational vision for Stoke-on-Trent which Robert Cant and others strove to bring about. When its Sixth Form College opened, there were only 11 Sixth Form Colleges in the whole of the country. Alderman Harold Naylor, told the Prime Minister, "We are confident that we are providing education opportunities for the youth of the city which cannot be excelled by any other authority in the United Kingdom."

The new College cost £500,000 to build. It was constructed in the style of many of the new

*Above: The programme that was produced to accompany the official opening of the Sixth Form College in 1970. **This picture:** An early view of the College.*

to eliminate the school atmosphere; he saw this very much as a half-way stage in the big step from school to the very different world of university. As Miss D Ball, his deputy, said, sixth formers often felt out of place in schools; at 18 when they were young adults with the right to vote. The new Sixth Form College recognised this, aiming to give the students

universities, in brick and concrete with soft timber panelling and wood block floors. Facilities were excellent, including a vast library on the first floor, general and specialist classrooms, tutorial space, lecture theatres and individual study bays. Science laboratories included a radio-active area, a dark room and an animal house. There were common rooms and a committee room for the students' use, kitchen and dining rooms, medical inspection facilities, changing rooms and showers, as well as staff common rooms and administrative offices including a college counsellor's room. The eight acre playing field area catered for many sports including cricket, running, jumping, discuss and shot putting, and provided two all-weather surface pitches. Visitors to the new Sixth Form College immediately noticed that it gave the impression of being "a mini-university", and this was no accident; the building was deliberately designed along the lines of the new universities to eliminate the school atmosphere. Mr H Beynon, the first Principal of the new College, had wanted

more freedom and personal responsibility, closer relationships with their teachers, and opportunities to have a voice in the running of their College.

The College was planned to accommodate 1,250 students aged 16 to19, who would have progressed from infants' schools (aged 5 to 8) to middle schools (8 to 12) and through non-selective high schools (12 to 16). A wide range of A-level subjects were on offer at the College, and the emphasis was on preparing students for entry to universities and other higher educational establishments. The great advantage of concentrating A-level teaching in a single establishment was, of course, economy of resources, both

*Above: A group of students photographed to commemorate the new intake. **Right:** Students studying in the library in the early 70s.*

Hall complex was completed in 1998.

To date, the College has only seen three new Principals; the first Principal, Harold Beynon, retired in 1972 and was succeeded by Syd Brown who served until 1985. His successor, Robert Stephenson, remained in office until 1993 when the fourth and current Principal Christina Cassidy was appointed. The Government has published two reports on the College, an HM Inspectorate Report in 1984 whilst Syd Brown was Principal, and an FEFC Inspection Report in 1996 under the present Principal. Both reports were extremely favourable. The 1984 report commented that the College was well staffed, soundly organised, efficiently administered and firmly led, and concluded that "academic achievements and personal qualities of the students reflect great credit

equipment and teachers, and it meant that the less popular A-level options which not all schools had been able to offer could now be taught more effectively with larger groups of students from all over the City. All these precepts are of course widely recognised in the late 1990s, but when the Sixth Form College first opened they were very new ideas, described by Harold Wilson as a remarkably creative experiment. Stoke's commitment to the provision of first-class education was rewarded by impressive examination results from its first intake of students, an achievement which has been repeated year after year thanks to the high standard of teaching and the supportive environment of the College.

Plans to extend the College were in hand as soon as it opened, with a new Social Studies block being constructed in 1975. Further significant improvements to the accommodation were made in 1994 when corridors were widened, a new reception area was built and the laboratories were re-modelled. Since then, an on-going programme of improvements has included refurbishment of all teaching areas including lecture theatres, laboratories and the multi-media resource area, and significant remodelling of student social areas to provide more space and an attractive place in which to relax. The Sports

*Top: Students working on ceramics in one of the well-equipped art and craft studios. **Right:** Principal Mrs Christina Cassidy, officially launching the scheme to upgrade the swimming pool and build two new sports halls in 1997.*

on the principal and staff". The more recent report acknowledges the College's ranking amongst the top third of further education colleges in the country in its AS and A-level results in 1994/5; it praises the quality of teaching, the organisation of the courses and the College's strategic plan and administrative efficiency as well as student guidance and support.

A recent development in the range of the College's teaching activities has been the provision of adult education. Whilst being a useful source of additional funding towards the building programme, this has also strengthened the College's links with the local community, and indeed the 1996 Report highlights "the excellent community links and valuable partnerships with local organisations" as one of the main strengths of the College. The College has become an active member of the Stoke-on-Trent Community Partnership, the Staffordshire Partnership, Stoke-on-Trent Common Purpose and the North Staffordshire Chamber of Commerce and Industry. In 1998 students of the College created a series of spectacular sculptures out of redundant materials provided by British Steel; these were exhibited at the Potteries Shopping Centre before being moved to a site alongside the Trent and Mersey Canal, and the project was praised by Arts Minister Mark Fisher.

As well as budding sculptors, the College has produced its share of famous people. Sports personalities include footballer Lee Chapman, cricketer

Dominic Cork, golfers David Lynne and Lisa Hackney, and Great Britain and Olympic hockey player Imran Sherwani. Neil Morrissey of television's 'Men Behaving Badly' is a former Stoke-on-Trent Sixth Form College student, as is Timothy Hugh, the internationally famous cellist, who returned to play at the 25th Anniversary Musical Celebration of the College in 1995.

The College now caters for some 1,700 students, and is one of the largest and most successful sixth form colleges in the country. Stoke-on-Trent is justifiably proud of the College which it set up almost thirty years ago when the concept of sixth form colleges was new. When Mr Wilson performed the opening ceremony in 1970 he made just one criticism of the new Sixth Form College - that the response to it had been "almost too enthusiastic", and both students and the community at large are still just as enthusiastic about the College today.

Top right: Two students appearing in 'The Importance of Being Earnest', in 1995, one of the many dramatic productions staged by the College's Drama Department.
Left: Students using the state-of-the-art information technology facilities.

A sizzling success

After the Second World War during which he had served in the RAF, James Blakeman spent a short time as manufacturing supervisor with a pork butcher in Leek, Staffordshire.

Having picked up what he needed to know about the business he decided to set up on his own. He started small, taking a mobile refreshment bar in partnership with his brother in law and, at the same time, worked as a freelance sausagemeat manufacturer.

After his marriage in 1955, Jim bought a farm near Stoke-on-Trent, turning cow sheds and stables at the back into a small manufacturing set-up for sausage, cooked meats and poultry. It was a modest enterprise, turning out 100 lbs. of sausage per week on small, hand-operated machines. Soon, though, he moved up into large quantity production with an Alexander Werk filler and a Seydlemann bowl chopper. The weekly sausage production at the farm soon topped the three-ton mark.

Since then, Blakemans moved to factory number two at Northam Road, Hanley, spending several thousands of pounds on larger machinery, including mincers, fillers and massagers. The sound of all this machinery was no longer to be heard on the farm but took pride of place in 1977 in the modern factory at Northam Road. Thanks to an 80-litre version of the Alpina bowl cutter the firm began to produce more than seven tons of sausage per week. The range covered Supreme Quality Sausages and a Catering Sausage. There was even a deep- fry version for distributing to chip shops, canteens and motorway restaurants. In addition the company prepared a range of cooked meats.

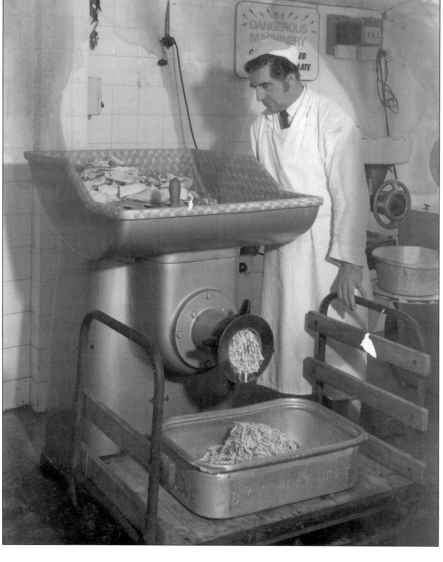

Top: First market stall Hanley general 1954. Left: One of the first production machines on the farm 1960.

The firm covered a 100 mile radius from Stoke and, during the summer season, products are taken by customers as far away as Cornwall. Blakemans moved in 1988 to showpiece premises in Trubshaw Cross, Longport. At this £650,000 self contained factory Blakemans has a clinically hygienic open plan layout with a working area of some 40,000 sq.ft.

Restructured as a Limited company this family concern set its sights on export provision. They became full European trading partners. Unfortunately, under EEC ruling Blakemans traditionally buoyant cooked meat business was incompatible within the same premises. Today the cooked meats are necessarily processed elsewhere.

The firm's EEC appointment, setting the highest standards possible for quality and hygiene within the food industry is complimented by their membership of the British Frozen Food Federation, the Institute of

Meat and the in-house training in Advanced Food Hygiene. Quality and Hygiene are as much a part of the ingredients of a Blakemans Sausage as the prime products and the secret seasoning they contain. Ever since James Blakeman, thirty-seven years ago, hit on the right mix of this and that to produce that special something that gives the sausage its special taste, the formula has been kept under lock and key.

Above: Poultry processing on the farm 1960.
Below: The fleet at Caverswall Farm 1960.

The business has come a long way from the back of the farm, but Blakemans insist on keeping close relations with all staff and senior management. They also enjoy personal involvement with all their long established customers.

Having worked for forty years in the business, Mrs Blakeman has now retired, but Mr Blakeman is acting Chairman and has over the past 50 years worked in, and completed all aspects of the entire meat trade, and claimed experience in buying from cattle markets, to slaughtering to general butchering, and on to the companies present skills in all types of meat manufacture. Both members of the younger generation hold key positions in the company, these being son Philip as Managing Director and daughter Susan as Finance Director. In addition to family the Blakemans employ a workforce of 50 who deal with sausage production, packaging and deliveries using vehicles from the firm's first class fleet.

Presently Blakemans supply sausages to any place where the Brits follow the sun, from Ibiza to Athens, from Denmark to Jersey and of course, throughout the UK. It has been estimated that in the nineties Blakemans manufacture enough sausages in a year to stretch from Tunbridge Wells to

Timbuktu and in five years to string round the world. From humble beginnings Blakemans now produce, on average, 220 tons of Supreme Sausage per week which equates to 4.8 million individual sausages.

Asked about plans for the future, the management says that it looks forward to many more years of continued success with the help of its willing and dedicated staff.

Above: The modern fleet of delivery vehicles.
Below: The board comprising family members Susan, Philip, Mr Blakeman and his wife Agnes.

An excellent service with quality products

Frank Albert Keeling was born in Newcastle, Staffordshire in 1880, the youngest of a large family. He married May Fielding, the daughter of Abram Fielding, founder of crown Devon Pottery.

Mr Keeling started a potter's merchant business on land belonging to his father-in-law and established Keeling & Walker (Walker being his mother's maiden name) which was incorporated as a limited company in 1916.

An office block of an innovative frame construction was built on the corner of Whieldon Road and Sutherland Street and is still the main office today.

During the 1914-18 war millions of dust respirators were produced by Keeling & Walker for use in the munitions factories (see photograph below) and in the 20's and early 30's Mr Keeling further developed the business through major agencies, particularly for ball clays from Dorset and the manufacture of Zinc Oxide.

Towards the end of this period, Mr Keeling identified a growing demand for Tin Oxide and established a new production facility on the site. Although this business did not prosper during the 1939-45 war years, as tin metal was required for more strategic purposes, it grew rapidly thereafter, becoming the company's principal activity.

In 1945 Mr Keeling was joined by bis son-in-law Mr Guy German, who developed a thriving export business, and in 1947 the company was further strengthened by association with a tin smelting company, the forerunner of the present owners, the Amalgamated Metal Corporation.

Mr Keeling died in 1958 aged 78 and the following year Mr David German joined his father, Guy, in the business, continuing the family connection into the 1990s.

Keeling & Walker has maintained a consistent development programme, with investment in buildings, technical resources, process technology, quality systems, and most recently in 1998, acquired the business of a major competitor in Germany.

As the largest producer of Tin Oxides worldwide, Keeling & Walker's strategy for the future is firmly based in its traditional values of customer service and product quality.

Above: A very early brochure displaying Keeling and Walker's wares. Below: Female staff making dust respirators for the munitions factories during World War I.

The hallmark company

Acme Marls is one of the world's leading design and development companies, dedicated to the manufacture and supply of an internationally renowned range of kiln furniture. Its range is comprehensive, catering for the sanitaryware, tableware, tiles, heavy clays and specialist ceramic industries.

It was founded in 1932 by J W A Lovatt. The scope of the organisation at that time was to process clays (marls) and later to pulverise them. It employed just eleven men and an office girl. The marl was sold to the local potters to make saggars in which to fire their wares. Acme Marls concentrated on supplying local pottery firms with Saggar Marl. A saggar is a clay box in which pottery is packed for firing. Saggars were used by potters to protect their clean ware from the effects of a dirty firing fuel, coal. The Company decided that it could make the saggars and sell them as a finished article. Two teams of saggar makers were employed, each consisting of three men. The saggar maker's frame filler would make the sides of the saggar. The saggar maker's bottom knocker would make the base and the saggar maker himself would 'weld' the base to the sides with clay. After drying, the saggar would be fired in a bottle oven and then delivered to the potter.

This venture was so successful that new and larger premises had to be found. An old established teapot manufacturer had just vacated a site in Bournes Bank in Burslem and Acme Marls moved in. The bottle ovens were ideal for the firing of saggars. As demand increased, it became possible to produce them by machine.

The period after the Second World War saw changes in the firing methods of pottery. Coal fired bottle ovens were slowly being replaced by long, gas fired tunnel kilns and the traditional saggar had to be replaced by a more open type of setting.

Mr Lovatt developed a new refractory material that could be pressed by machines in the form of a

Top: *An analysis report.*
Left: *A Saggar Maker assembling a base and side.*

*Left: An early Annealing Kiln. **Bottom left:** Saggars being placed into a Bottle Kiln. **Bottom right:** The forerunner of todays open placing system replacing the need for saggars.*

increased demand both at home and abroad. This was probably the last bottle oven to be built in the area and can still be seen today, with two sister ovens at Bournes Bank.

Since then Acme Marls has developed many other firsts. Notable amongst these was the development and manufacture of Dust Pressed Batts and Extruded Props. These props are needed in tableware firing. Objects varying in size from egg cups to coffee pots might all be placed on the same kiln car so that flexibility of placing heights is essential. Using Acme Marls' adjustable prop systems, with their slide-in, intermediate batts, or shelves, the problem of accommodating variable ware heights on the same kiln car is eliminated.

Manufacturers of products of similar ware heights would employ the company's fixed prop systems in order to have maximum kiln efficiency, loading levels and respective product yields.

shelf or batt. The design of propping systems enabled these batts to be supported as they took the potters' wares through their kilns. A bottle oven to fire these batts was built in the 1940s to meet the

and more land was obtained on which Acme Marls could build its own tunnel kiln. This method of firing became very popular, but kiln wrecks were a problem, when ware sometimes fell off the kiln car trucks during their passage through the kiln. On at least one occasion, when a wreck occurred, Mr Lovatt used a 303 rifle from his war service with the Royal Artillery to shoot out the wreck very successfully.

During the sixties Mr Lovatt's three sons joined the business. John and David are still with the company. Increased production meant that additional kilns were built in 1967 and 1973. During that period, the company purchased its die makers, Scotia Dies Ltd, which, with its blacksmithing works, J T Salts, now forms the Engineering branch of the Acme Marls Group.

In the late sixties, they were also the first company to introduce Adjustable Placing Systems.

Therefore, with firing still representing approximately one third of the cost of the product, correctly tailored placing systems are crucial to kiln efficiency. The development of dust pressing technology still represents the biggest innovation in the industry, even today.

By the early 1950s Acme Marls had invented the first Profile Setter for Bone China-Biscuit Placing. By 1953, demand for batts and a complete range of kiln furniture was outstripping supply

Top Left: Earthenware glost open firing.
Centre right: David and John Lovatt.
Right: Rob Harris, Managing Director (second right) and John Lovatt (right) receiving the ISO 9001 Award from Jim Leake (left) and Wilfred Heide (second left).

wide range of accessories such as placing stools, vanity basin setters and angle supports.

Extruded batts and props are hollow. They give the same performance as solid ones of the same dimensions, but, being only half the weight, they can be heated faster, using less energy with more even heating of the ware. They also allow for greater loading of the kiln.

Sanitaryware stools are used to vary the placing height of a fixed car deck, to enable products to rest vertically, thereby making optimum use of the available placing area. The stools are mainly used in the placing of water closets. They have a Flat Pack, self assembly design allowing for economical transportation and storage and the systems can be customised.

Acme Marls has emerged as a market-driven company based on ISO 9001 quality management and is also accredited to the Investors in People program. It is a company that seeks solutions and is led by the requirements of its customers. It has a market knowledge, quality, resource and technology base that is probably unsurpassed anywhere in the world today.

This, together with the firm's Interlocking Design Structure, instantly removed the need for cement which had been a constant source of contamination.

In 1976 a 20-acre site on the former Coal Board sidings in Tunstall was acquired and a new, single storey factory was built the following year. It is on this site, alongside the Greenway which follows the old railway track, that most of the company's products are now manufactured.

Acme Marls has consistently exported between 60% and 70% of its products to a world-wide market. Product design has been continuously improved so that Acme's original 'marl' production has now been replaced by the efficient manufacture of high-grade refractory products. The present board, consisting of family and non-family members, has built on the company's original values and spirit of innovation so that the name of Acme Marls is well known within today's international ceramic industry.

Sanitary ware kiln furniture designs vary considerably, from multi-deck Batt and Prop systems for conventional tunnel kilns, to those designed with light-weight furniture for fast firing processes. Acme Marl support their systems with a

Top Left: The current board of directors.
Below: Extruded Batts.

The company founded on opportunity

F G Chambers & Co Ltd was founded in 1906 by Frederick Gordon Chambers, a native of Hull, who came to Stoke to collect an outstanding debt on behalf of his employers but saw the opportunity to develop a timber business in North Staffordshire. The original site was located at Shelton Wharf railway sidings where a variety of English hardwoods was stored and trade gradually grew, giving the opportunity in 1924 to move to premises at Copeland Street, some 400 yards away from the original site.

Accent had now switched from hardwood to imported softwood with the main customer base being the local pottery, mining and engineering industries. Softwood became a very scarce item during and immediately after World War II and in fact was only allowed to be sold by fairly strict licence control

until 1954. During this time plywood was introduced as a major stock item free from licence control, and this proved to be the forerunner of considerable development in the following years into sheet material with such products as chipboard, laminates and more recently MDF.

As the range of products and the customer base continued to expand, adjoining premises in Copeland Street, together with land and buildings which became available in Vernon Road, were purchased to create more space for stock.

The Vernon Road site was only some 400 yards away from the main premises but was separated by two major roads and

Above: Frederick Gordon Chambers, founder of the Company. Below: Shelton Wharf railway sidings - where it all began.

transfer of stock and personnel proved to be a major headache.

Before the opening of the M6 in Staffordshire during the mid 1960s, plans had been made for a link road running through Stoke on Trent joining J15 and J16. This was to become known locally as the D Road but it did impose a planning blight in the centre of Stoke for many years. This restricted development of the Company until agreement was

Above: The timber sheds at Copeland Street.
Right: FG Chambers' offices in Copeland Street to which the company moved in 1924.

reached to purchase a greenfield site of just under five acres in North Street, to which the Company moved in 1973.

By a good stroke of timing Perstorp Warerite, whose product range was now equal to that of Formica, introduced a large sheet size of laminate, 4120 x 1540mm, which was attractive to large users but difficult for many distributors to hold in stock, due to the common problem of shortage of space. Utilising the new facility to its maximum the full range of this laminate was placed into stock and offered to other distributors throughout the UK in smaller quantities than they could purchase ex Perstorp. This led FG Chambers into national distribution for the first time in its history and shortly afterwards the consolidation of the booming DIY market started with the appearance of National Groups taking the place of a myriad of smaller shops. Chambers was then in an excellent position to service this rapidly growing industry with a wide range of wood based products which included planed softwood, hardboard, plywood, chipboard, doors and worktops.

The North Street site had been envisaged, at the time of purchase, to cope with normal expansion for the foreseeable future but the success of the

Chambers range offered to the DIY majors exceeded all expectations and a search for larger premises was instigated in the mid 1980s, culminating in the purchase of the old West Midlands Gas Board site in Etruria.

This was a site of 11.5 acres and clearance commenced in late 1986 with a final move from North Street taking place in 1989.

It had been the wish of the Directors to construct a timber building but the requirements of a 50 metre clear span proved too difficult for the timber engineering industry to meet at this particular time. However, subsequent improvements in technology have made this possible.

This fourth(and possibly last) home for Chambers was less than a mile away from the original humble beginnings and indeed all four bases were within a short distance of each other. The Etruria site houses the largest single industrial building built in Stoke on Trent since 1945 and comprises the most up-to-date racking, handling and distribution techniques available to the trade. Full computer systems have been in place for several years and are updated on a regular basis

Above: The Company's North Street premises.

to take advantage of any improvements available.

Upon moving to Etruria operations commenced on a 24 hour basis to enable Chambers to deliver the bulk of the orders over a great part of the country on a 24 hour turnaround to meet the newly discovered customer requirement of 'just in time'.

In 1996 the Board of Directors chaired by Gordon Bruce Chambers - the son of the founder- accepted an offer from management and investment bankers for the purchase of the business but the Chambers family have continued to maintain a shareholding in the Company and follow its development with great interest.

*Above: The Etruscan Street premises in a picture dating from 1989. **Left:** The West Midlands Gas Board site before the Company took it over in the mid 1980s.*

A century of service to the facilities management industry

It was in 1895 that the first hammer in George Scarr Hall's workshop struck hot metal on his £2.00 anvil. Since that day, the ethos of the company has not changed. The workforce were - and still are - hand-picked for their excellence in particular skills. As industrial black-smiths, they installed and maintained equipment in a variety of industrial settings. Using the anvil, hammer, furnace and steel tubes, they made straps to go round bottle ovens. They provided all the local potteries with heating systems for high pressure hot water boiler plant made by George S. Hall's. From their premises in Town Road, where the head office still is, they were encouraged to make, deliver and accept only the best.

Hanley provided the ideal location for George Scarr Hall's business. Alongside the local industry, Mr Hall's business prospered and he expanded its customer base, providing a wider range of building maintenance services.

The World Wars, particularly the second, took many skilled men away from the firm, though exemption was given to men working on Ministry of Defence sites. The recession of the thirties too caused some problems for George S. Hall's as local firms were in difficulties and could not afford their services.

Top: George Scarr Hall in his workshop 100 years ago. Left: George Scarr Hall, company founder, left, Arthur Sturgess, blacksmith, fourth from left, with members of staff, pictured manhandling a high pressure hot water boiler manufactured by the Company for installation in one of the local potteries. Below: Hanley in 1895.

customers' premises and equipment. Computerised maintenance programmes are set up to ensure optimum performance. Throughout the United Kingdom, Europe and the USA George S Hall has been awarded contracts from banks, hotels, retail chains, building societies, local and national government authorities and hospitals in both the public and private sector. Examples of these clients are The Automobile Association, PricewaterhouseCoopers, Barclay's Bank, Tesco, Boots and the Royal Bank of Scotland.

George Scarr Hall senior died in 1944 and Mr Joseph Henshall joined the Board of Directors alongside Mr Hall's son, also George. The company has remained a family run business to this day, with the current Chairman, Mr Ian Scarr Hall being the founder's grandson and his two sons also work for the Company.

The Service and Maintenance Division opened in 1969 and, in 1982, in order to concentrate on this, the contracting involvement was ceased.

GEO. S. HALL LTD.
HEATING ENGINEERS
HIGH STREET & BOW STREET
HANLEY, STOKE ON TRENT
PHONE STOKE-ON-TRENT 5064

Whilst, in terms of technology, the business is unrecognisable compared with that of a century ago, the provision of total customer satisfaction has remained the company's central concern. For the remainder of this century and into the next George S. Hall will continue to invest in people and technology to maintain their position at the leading edge of the facilities management industry.

Over the last 100 years dramatic changes have been experienced in the engineering and technology requirement of the facilities management profession. Now the company purchases energy for its customers, innovating monitoring devices for measuring the electrical quantities needed by

Top: The company's premises at Town Road in the early years. Above: A plaque cast at George S. Hall's forge. Below: A fleet of vehicles lined up in 1962.

Total transfer technology

Capper Rataud Limited is a global company which has a long tradition of manufacturing high quality transfers.

The roots of the company date back to 1905 with the founding of Rataud Limited. Brothers Pierre and Paul Rataud had had a ceramic transfers business in Limoges but decided that there was a better business opportunity in Stoke-on-Trent and subsequently relocated.

Then in 1920, Ben Capper, previously the works manager of a pottery business and well versed in its requirements, set himself up as a supplier to the pottery industry from premises on Wellesley Street, Shelton. It was in the 1920s that Rataud Limited and Ben Capper Limited began working closely together.

By the 1950s the company was playing an important role in revolutionising the ceramic industry with the introduction of Covercoat, to produce waterslide transfers for the very first time.

Later, in association with Automated Transfers Limited they developed the first truly practical method of applying transfers by heat release. The production and design of transfers for ceramic tiles are Capper's most recent success story.

The development of non-ceramic transfers which can be applied to a wide range of difficult shapes

and substrates, including coated metals, plastics, glass and wood is evidence of the company's constant search for new products. The teamwork between Ben Capper Limited and Rataud Limited continued until 1984 when the two companies merged to form Capper Rataud Limited. With the formulation of the new company, the expertise and technical knowledge of these two market leaders was shared, enabling Capper Rataud Limited to continue producing transfers which exemplify the very best in transfer printing.

The highly skilled in-house designers at Capper Rataud create a wide range of designs for their many customers, from exciting contemporary patterns to the traditional time-tested ones.

The company is careful to keep abreast of the rapid advancement of technology within the industry. Recently over half a million pounds was invested to computerise fully the origination department, enabling the company to scan designs electronically and store them on the computer system. The system operators can then adapt the designs to the exact requirements of the customers.

Top left: Paul A Rataud, who founded Rataud Limited along with his brother Pierre. Top right: Ben Capper, proprietor of his own company providing supplies to the ceramic industry. Above: An early Rataud memo.

have the support of the best technical expertise within the industry.

The relationship between the company and its customers has always been considered to be of the utmost importance. For example in the early 1920s, the directors of Rataud Limited received a complaint from Johnson Brothers concerning a late delivery. A board meeting was called to discuss the problem and it was discovered that the undertaker, who also worked as the delivery man, was unable to catch his horse on the morning in question. It therefore became company policy to tether the horse during the week in order to ensure prompt deliveries. Although over the years methods have changed, the attitudes within the company have not. This is highlighted by the way in which the company undertook a vigorous quality assurance programme resulting in its coveted BS 5750 ISO9001, which guarantees constant and consistent high quality.

As Capper Rataud Ltd approaches the new millennium and its own centenary celebrations the company confidently looks forward to a continuing bright future. Based solidly on its philosophy of Total Transfer Technology, Capper Rataud will continue to develop new products and services that will ensure it maintains its well-respected place in a rapidly evolving industrial marketplace.

Top right: Some of the staff enjoying their Christmas Party in 1948. *Top left:* A printing machine being moved from the Stoke factory to the new Hanley factory in 1968. *Below:* The 90s Board of Capper Rataud, pictured from left to right: Back row: James Capper, Jeff Hardman, Malcolm Robertson, Ian Townley. Front row: Michael Capper (Managing Director), Philip Capper (Chairman).

An excellent customer support system ensures that someone from the company is always available to offer advice to clients. Ongoing research and development, with customer consultation and discussion, covers all aspects of production including design, colour, covercoats and the finished product. Consequently, when you buy a Capper Rataud transfer you can be assured that you will

The company that's had it taped for over 60 years

Selectus Limited, situated on the fringe of the former heart of the British textile industry, has its UK factory in the village of Biddulph, close to Stoke on Trent Founded in 1936, the company is a recognised pioneer in the haberdashery and fastenings industry.

It can claim many firsts in the manufacture of products that are taken for granted now as a part of everyday life.

Its roots lie with the Senn family from Basle in Switzerland. Its sons worked for a ribbon manufacturer whose firm they took over at the turn of the century. So, Senn & Company came into being. It demonstrated flair and innovation from the start, being the first Swiss ribbon company to use artificial silk, later developed as rayon and viscose.

The fourth generation of Senns turned this family firm into a Limited Liability Company in 1928.

At this time the company patented seamless bias binding and formed two subsidiary companies, one of which, Selectus Ltd, was based in London.

In 1931 Britain introduced duties on textile imports, hitting what had been a core market for Senn, and the decision was taken to open a UK factory to manufacture ribbon. Biddulph was chosen as the ideal location because of its proximity to other textile towns such as Macclesfield, Leek and Congleton. The other factor was the available workforce in the area. The first plant was built by 1936. In the same year, Gustav Senn emigrated to the UK and by July weaving had begun on the site. Equipment included shuttle looms and manual winders. Raw materials were mainly cotton, silk, rayon and triacetate.

Throughout the war years Selectus continued to manufacture ribbons and other products, returning to using real silk since viscose was scarce. Following the war the company was thriving to the extent that it was able to build 76 houses adjacent to the factory to help Britain's post-war rebuilding effort. When completed, most were sold to the local council.

In 1949 Selectus adopted its familiar 'Panda' brand for its range of ribbons, including an eye-catching giant panda logo that

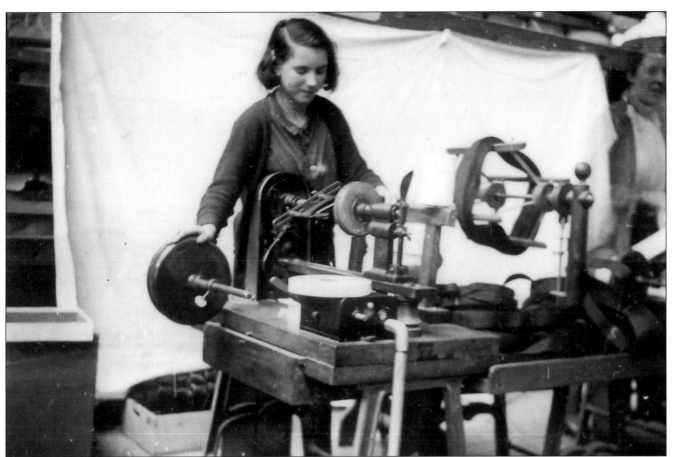

remains very well known today. At the cutting edge of the industry, Selectus became the first ribbon manufacturer to use Terylene polyester fibre in satin ribbon. A much more significant development was the appointment of Selectus in 1956 as the sole UK and Ireland licensee for the manufacture and sale of a revolutionary new fastener, Velcro, invented by swiss businessman George de Mestral.

Velcro hook and loop fastener was first marketed in the UK in 1960, under the managing directorship of Peter Senn, son of Gustav. It was an immediate success. In 1962 Selectus acquired ownership of the Velcro fastener trademark for the UK and Ireland. As the company expanded rapidly it invested more of its profits into developing the Velcro fastener. A £1 million project was begun to build a modern dyehouse in 1974, overseen by current chairman and Managing director Dieter Senn. Soon 240 people were working in the much-extended Biddulph

Above: An advertisement for Velcro.
Top: A worker in the 1940s.
Right: The old finishing room in the 1950s.
Facing page, top left: The founder, Gustav Senn.
Facing page, top right: An early advertisement for one of the company's products.
Facing page, bottom: Setting up the weaving shed in 1936.

premises, its products being found in many applications including packaging, clothing, aircraft and furniture.

The present factory has high speed needle looms, continuous dyeing and finishing, automatic winding, electronic controls and monitoring, all a far cry from that first factory opened in Biddulph in 1936. The yarns though are pretty much the same except that silk is no longer used.

The company's main customers are leading retailers, car manufacturers and national industrial distributors. Their products are bought as far afield as the USA, Australasia, Europe and Scandinavia. The company plans to grow the markets in which it operates through product and application development and to develop new markets for its products and manufacturing resources.

There is no lack of imagination behind these plans. Two years ago, a false leg, stuck on with a Velcro strap saved the life of an injured duckling.

The mallard was taken to the Norfolk Seal and Bird Rescue Trust when he was found injured on the road. One of his legs had to be amputated. His other leg was not strong enough to support him which meant his plumage would have become irretrievably damaged.

A prosthetic surgeon from Sellyoak Hospital, Birmingham designed a false limb for him, to be strapped on with Velcro. Now the duck is able to stand for up to half an hour each day, saving his plumage and his life. Selectus is paying for his upkeep at the Trust and donating free Velcro straps for life!

According to Dieter Senn, 'There's Fred the hedgehog who also had a false leg attached with Velcro and a horse that apparently had its tail stuck back on....' Not quite what George de Mestral had in mind.

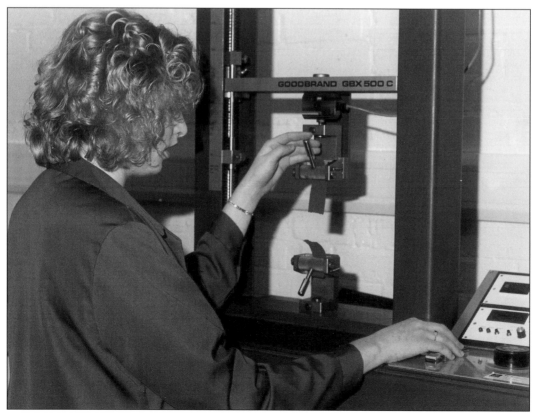

Above: The weaving shed today.
Left: Velcro testing.

Serving the world's leading ceramic producers

In 1867 a potter, William Tunnicliff, and a toolmaker, Thomas Taylor, went into partnership. They set up a specialised pottery to serve the Birmingham metal industries at a premises in Broad Street, Shelton, Hanley.

There, using pugmills, lathes, driers and kilns, they worked on clays, fluxes and flint to fashion door furniture, lamp holders, tobacco jars and photographic developing equipment. Mr Taylor was happy to apply his engineering skills to pottery, an element of precision being necessary because of the products' association with metal parts.

When the firm outgrew the factory at Shelton, much larger premises were taken at Eastwood. There was a rapid increase in demand for electricity following World War 1 and trade increased for Taylor-Tunnicliff when the electricity industry required insulators to withstand the increased distribution voltage. After the retirement of Mr Tunnicliff in 1895 a private limited company, Taylor, Tunnicliff and Co. Ltd. was formed.

Meanwhile, as far back as 1840 a small family pottery business had been started by Mr John Buller in Bovey Tracy in Devon. It made kiln furniture that was bought by the potteries in North Staffordshire. It seemed logical that Bullers should move from Devon and they settled at Hanley in Stoke on Trent. Here, this company too produced electrical insulators and, by 1868, was making them complete with ironwork.

In 1885 Bullers bought the metal foundry of Jobson Brothers at Tipton and Buller, Jobson & Company Ltd was formed. In 1890 it had become Bullers Ltd.

So it was that whilst the electrical age was in its infancy both companies had embarked on the specialised production of insulators. Bullers built a new factory at Milton, just outside the Potteries where production began in 1920. Taylor Tunnicliff erected a new factory at Stone in Staffordshire which opened two years later. They also bought a factory at Longton and this plant was used for the production of ceramic refractory formers, needed for electric fires, cookers and other heating appliances. Yet another factory was acquired at Hanley in 1928

Below: Women staff in the testing Laboratory, carrying out a routine mechanical test.

and devoted to small turned ware and die pressed insulators.

World War 2 brought the company high priority demands for specialised ceramics to be used in RADAR and other high powered communications. Bullers' factory at Milton and Taylor Tunnicliffs' at Stone were both designed for the production of high voltage insulators. Enlargement had been necessary at both plants to keep up with demand for even larger insulators. Taylor Tunnicliff completed a seies of extensions at Stone in 1951. By the time Bullers' expansion programme was completed in 1967 the two firms had already done the logical thing and amalgamated, to become Allied Insulators Limited.

Throughout the 1970s, the expansion programme continued under a new holding company, A1 Industrial Products plc., with acquisitions in Surrey, Walsall and Leeds. However with the 1980s recession, the company was broken up, and the various divisions sold to new owners. The small insulator business passed to its current owners and continued its operations under the former company name of Taylor, Tunnicliff Ltd.

Above: A section of the pressing shop.
Right: Comparing brick drawn during the firing, with the reading of the Ring.

Today, the major product of Taylor Tunnicliff Ltd is Bullers Rings. These are marketed and used worldwide in the monitoring of kiln firing of most types of ceramic goods from bricks to high tech ceramics.

The precise date of the invention of Bullers Rings is not clear, but an article in the Pottery Gazette in 1905 very accurately describes both Bullers Rings and the gauge used to measure shrinkage. Taylor Tunnicliff still possesses an early gauge which exactly matches the drawing of the gauge in the article. The author claimed successfully to have introduced the use of rings and the measuring device at 'one of the principal manufactories in the Potteries' some five years earlier. The company likes to think this was Bullers. Whether or not, Bullers Rings were obviously in use from about 1900.

In earlier years, before the use of electrical and now electronic instruments, Bullers Rings were used as the only means of controlling firings. Nowadays sophisticated instruments perform the control duties, but the assessment of sufficiency and uniformity of the fire can only be done by Bullers Rings and similar devices.

Bullers Rings are simple and easy to use, giving assessment of firing as a unique number, recognised worldwide. Sales continue to rise, and because of their high quality, reliability and consistency, Bullers Rings have become the industry standard, and have helped build the Ceramics Industry as we know it today.

*Above: The Jolly Shop. **Below:** Taylor and Tunnicliff's exhibition stand circa 1955.*

He who works prospers

The company of S Keeling has been well known in Etruria since 1974 but it has a far longer history. Thomas Keeling, the father of the dynasty, embarked on several business ventures. They included buying the Queens Hotel in Hanley which unfortunately failed when the new railway line that was to bring customers missed the site by miles. The hotel was sold

to the Corporation at a considerable loss to the Keelings and the building became the town hall and renamed the Victoria Hall. Thomas Keeling's initials can still be seen on the Bagnall Street side of it. Next, Mr Keeling invested in watercress beds at Waterhouses which were also a financial failure. In despair, Thomas Keeling bought an island off Vancouver, taking two sons and leaving behind his wife, another son Sam and one daughter.

Sam and his mother invested in timber selling and in a short time had first established and then extended the firm. The business, in Copeland Street, Stoke, was inherited by Sam's son Geoffrey. It remained and flourished here until the motorway Queensway was proposed. A move was necessary because of compulsory purchase but Geoffrey's son, another Sam, had great difficulty in persuading his father to move in advance of the premises being required, especially as the new site, when it was first purchased, was a complete wilderness. Two pubs were demolished to make way for the new buildings. The company's original brass plate was put up in the entrance hall.

Once the move had been made Geoffrey Keeling was prouder than ever of the new headquarters in Forge Lane. The new road which had forced the firm out of its old home gave it better communications. In the same year as the move, 1973, Sam's son David joined the firm.

In Forge Lane the timber firm became heavily mechanised. The mid seventies saw the rise of the National Garden Festival

Top: Sam Keeling was a little boy when his dad left to go to Vancouver, Sam is pictured as a grown up with his family, the little boy is Geoffrey.
Left: Copeland Street - Sid Stockley wood machinist operating state of the art Bandsaw.

which enhanced the area and brought millions of people, potential customers for Keelings, to the site.

By the mid eighties the firm had three huge storage sheds containing timber from all over the world. Spruce and plywood came from Canada and British Columbia but the best timber came from north Russia. This had been slowly grown in cold conditions and was easy to work because it was dense with fewer knots and a straighter grain. Mahogany came from Africa, Brazil and the Philippines.

Keelings' timber is stacked to a height of 30 feet, using side loaders to lay the planks as straight and flat as possible to prevent twisting. The ends of planks are coded with stars, letters and numbers to indicate place of origin and grade of timber.

Keelings opened a treatment plant in 1979 to protect wood against fungal decay and wet and dry rot. They bought plant and chemicals from Rentokil and worked in conjunction with them. The chemicals were not brushed on but the wood was impregnated using a pressure system of 180 lbs to the square inch. Later a flame retardant treatment was also begun.

So that the firm remains popular with its neighbours, its huge saws are soundproofed. Blades uses for softwood are renewed every few days. Those used for teak or mahogany are renewed much more often. In 1985 Keelings acquired a computer controlled moulder into which rough wood could be fed, coming out as a smooth product. Progress was made in the office. old hand written ledgers were replaced by a comput-

erised accounting system which deals with all aspects of sales purchasing and stock control.

Keelings' workforce often works to architects' drawings, the finished product being sent out to the required site to be used in construction but one-off handcarving jobs are still offered. The company's plan for the future is to continue to build on the firm foundation that has been built. Its achievements well illustrate the family motto, 'Floret qui labrat.' (He who works prospers.)

"I see our company continuing to consolidate its position locally as a reputable and reliable timber merchant," says director David Samuel Keeling, " We have an ongoing programme of modernisation and maintenance to improve our saw mill, timber treatment plant and distribution service so that our customers will also benefit."

"Environmental issues continue to dominate our source of supply and these markets are studied very closely during political, civil and climatic changes."

Top left: Harry Platt operating a spindle moulder.
Top right: Managing Director, Sam Keeling and his son, David. Below: Original buildings in Copeland Street from where they moved in 1973.

Beauty from ash, for fine bone china

Jesse Shirley & Son is a family-owned business, today able to proclaim itself the world's oldest and leading producer of calcined Bone Ash for the manufacture of fine bone china. The origins of this remarkable success story lie in a revolutionary development in the pottery industry at the end of the 18th century.

It was in the 1790s that Josiah Spode, when working on the problems associated with porcelain manufacture, first mixed kaolin, china-stone and bone ash (made from the calcined bones of cattle) to produce a white paste of even translucency which could be marketed at a reasonable price. This remarkable innovation brought into being an entirely new branch of pottery manufacture. At first called Stoke porcelain, it soon became known by the more familiar name of Bone China, thereby immortalising its distinctive ingredient: calcined Bone Ash.

The name of Jesse Shirley first appears in history in the early 1840s, on the payroll of a company called Messrs Bourne & Hudson - a business begun in 1820 to respond to the burgeoning demand for Bone Ash in the manufacture of the new china. Before bone can be ground effectively, it must first undergo two preparatory processes: firstly it must be degelatinised and then calcined in a kiln at a temperature in excess of 1,000°C - the result is a white material, with a specific crystalline structure, thereafter readily milled. Messrs Bourne & Hudson specialised in these two processes, at first renting and later acquiring a nearby mill to carry out the grinding process. Although Jesse Shirley's precise role in the business is not recorded, he must certainly have made his mark, for when John Bourne died in 1852 - after an illness 'borne with exemplary fortitude and Christian resignation' - Jesse and his brother Joseph inherited half of the estate. Jesse immediately took over the works' operation and, within a few short years, his enterprising vision, not to mention considerable capital investment, was reaping its rewards: in 1857 the Etruscan Flint and Bone Mill first opened its doors to a new era. The brainchild of Jesse Shirley, the mill was able to handle all aspects of Bone Ash production - including calcination and grinding -

*Above: Eldest son of the founder, the second Jesse Shirley, 1848-1927. **Below:** The workforce during the 1940s.*

on one site. Designed and built by the redoubtable George Kirk of Etruria, it boasted a two chamber calcining kiln, a pan room and gear room, a boiler house and an engine house housing an 1830s double acting beam engine, called 'Princess', steam-driven and reputedly built by J and T Sherratt of Salford. It is a testament to the foresight of Jesse Shirley, that - apart from some necessary updates over the years - the mill functioned successfully in this form for well over a century!

By 1880, Jesse's sons, Jesse and Henry Benjamin Shirley were running the company and establishing a family tradition which continues to this day - the flame of industry passing successively from father to son, from one generation to the next, to be kindled afresh in the light of each new age. Public service and a commitment to the local community were hallmarks of the Shirley family even in those early days. The younger Jesse was elected to Hanley Council in 1880; five years later he served as mayor and in 1892 became an alderman. His brother, meanwhile, was a Hanley Council member from 1893, mayor in 1902 and later President of Hartshill Cricket Club.

The 20th century has brought remarkable and dramatic developments to all manufacturing processes - revolutionary advances in technologies have generated challenging conditions for nearly all traditional industries - but for those up to the task it has also meant a time of unprecedented opportunity.

For Jesse Shirley, a period of transformation began in the early 1970s with the start of nearly three decades of reinvestment for the company, updating both production and research facilities and diversifying its product range to meet the challenges of new worldwide markets. The old mill, after long service, finally became redundant in 1972 and was superseded by state-of-the-art machinery and techniques developed elsewhere on site. Jesse Shirley now produces the finest quality calcined Bone Ash for a variety of customers all over the globe. The plant is technologically the most advanced of its kind and incorporates a production laboratory with specialist test equipment and a chemical analysis facility together with sophisticated computer control of high density magnet cleaning. Product diversification has ensured that Jesse Shirley now supplies a complete range of raw materials for Fine Bone China - including China Clays and Fluxes and spray dried granulates for isostatic pressing or back tempering - whilst an extensive programme of research has revealed

other applications for Bone Ash itself, notably in the glass and metal industries.

But what of the old mill? When it closed in 1972, it was the last steam driven potters' mill in Britain, a fact that earned it scheduling as an Ancient Monument in 1975. Soon afterwards, the staff of the Stoke-on-Trent City Museum, together with a team of volunteers embarked on an enthusiastic programme of restoration. The Mill now has a new lease of life as a fascinating industrial museum, and old 'Princess' is in steam on the first weekend of each month.

Jesse Shirley's ambitious investment in the 1850s paid off handsomely in his own time, and has secured a three-fold legacy in the Etruria of today - an illuminating embodiment of his original vision, in the form of the old mill; its present-day incarnation as a sophisticated, highly specialised, modern company; and, perhaps most important of all, his own descendants - one of whom, Mr J C M Shirley, stands today at the helm of this remarkable enterprise.

Above: Mr J C M Shirley, the current Managing Director of Jesse Shirley Ltd.

A winning formula - unchanged through the centuries

For more than two and a quarter centuries Spode china has been appreciated by connoisseurs and ordinary people alike, bought and treasured by collectors, and used throughout the world for daily meals and for banquets. Yet when Josiah Spode was set to work for twelve hours a day in a pottery at the age of seven, the year after his father had died and been buried in a pauper's grave, he could hardly have guessed that he destined to make Spode a household name for centuries to come.

It was in 1749, when Josiah was 16, that he took the first step in the direction which was to lead to fame and fortune. In that year he was apprenticed to Thomas Whieldon, who was at that time the most successful potter in Staffordshire. Five years later, after serving his apprenticeship, Josiah moved on to work as a skilled potter for William Banks of Stoke, and from there he went on to open his own small factory. He began by making cream-coloured and blue-painted earthenware, and his line was obviously popular because he was eventually able to buy the factory of his former employer, William Banks. Here he worked and experimented to find the best methods of making pottery. This site remains, to this day, the home of Spode.

Whilst Josiah Spode was developing his own skills, a great deal of experimentation with new

ceramic materials was being carried out in the Potteries in the search for a material which could be used for the manufacture of white tableware. Chinese painted blue and white designs had been imported in quantity and had become popular, but since the East India Company had begun to

Above: An illustration by Fortunio Matania depicting 'probably the most significant development in the history of English ceramics', Josiah Spode's first successful piece of bone china.

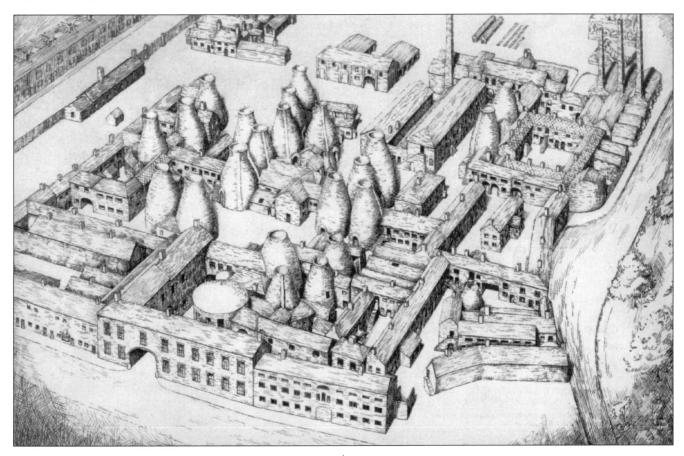

reduce their imports of chinaware in 1773 these items had become increasingly scarce. The potteries reproduced these designs by hand on the cream coloured ware of the time, but could not produce them in sufficient quantity to meet demand.

Josiah Spode perfected the process of blue under-glaze printing on earth-enware from hand-engraved copper plates, and this major breakthrough established his reputation. By 1784 he had won general acclaim for this achievement, and from then on the prosperity of his company was assured. But Josiah Spode was not content with this single achievement; he continued with his pioneering work, and in the closing years of the 18th century he was working to perfect the formula for making Fine Bone China.

Today, both Spode Blue and Fine Bone China are made in essentially the same way as they were two hundred years ago. Since 1984, most blue and white ware has been transfer printed onto white earth-enware. The Spode earth-enware body is still made with the 1820 ingre-dients of calcined flint, china stone, china clay and ball clay. The design is created initially on paper, then hand engraved on copper plates. This is a highly-skilled process. The engraved plate is heated, then filled with

Top: The Spode Works 1833-4, a drawing by Harold Holdway taken from an earthenware site model in the Spode Museum. *Above:* One of the many designs, this one from 1853, housed in Spode's unique pattern book archive.

away, leaving the design on the ware. Finally it is 'hardened on' in a kiln to remove the 'oils', before being glazed and fired to produce the rich, characteristic Spode blue, protected permanently under the glaze.

The first designs which Josiah Spode created using this process were reproductions of the Chinese porcelain designs and patterns in the Chinese idiom. But other patterns soon followed, including the earliest blue florals. Three patterns originally introduced between 1790 and 1820 are still produced today; these are Blue Italian, Tower Blue and Willow.

inorganic metallic oxides mixed with oils, wiped clean of excess pigment, and after wetting with a solution of soap and water a special tissue paper is laid on top. After passing through rollers to impress the paper onto the engraving, the tissue is peeled away to reveal the pattern in reverse. Cut out by hand, the tissue is carefully positioned before being rubbed down on the ware with a stiff-bristled brush. The whole piece is then immersed in running water and the tissue floats

The Spode factory still adheres equally faithfully to the original 18th century formula for its Fine Bone China. The raw ingredients are calcined bone, china clay and stone (china or Cornish). These are mixed with water in a 'blunger' before

Top left: King George V and Queen Mary pictured during their visit to the Spode factory in Stoke in 1913. *Below:* The print shop in 1926.

cup rims are cut by hand, and handles are cut to shape and attached by hand. After the initial biscuit firing, all table ware is glazed by hand before the glost firing. Then the various types of decoration are applied before the final firing, with special patterns and gilding applied by skilled artists.

It is often claimed that Spode's formula for Fine Bone China is the single most significant development in the history of the industry, as its brilliant whiteness and delicate translucency inspired new standards of artistry, skill and finish across the whole industry. There had been interest in the use of bone ash as a tableware ingredient from around 1750, and in fact it had been used in the middle ages in cupels for the assaying of metals. In the second half of the 18th century several experimental formulations were tried, but these were 'soft-paste' porce-

being purified and having a large proportion of the water removed in a filter press. After maturing for a few days, the clay passes through a pug mill to extract every bubble of air. 'Making' is divided into four main processes; flat making of plates, saucers,etc; cup making; pressing by hand of platters, open vegetable dishes, etc; and casting, again by hand, or holloware such as soup tureens, tea and coffee pots. The processes and techniques used at Spode today are essentially the same as those which Josiah Spode used, and because the amount of mechanisation that can be employed in the manufacturing process is so limited, a very high degree of artistry, hand work and craftsman skills are required throughout all stages of production. All scallops on

Above: Some of the tools required for engraving copper plates. **Top right:** *Paper and copper plate going through the press.* **Right:** *Paul Holdway engraving copper plates.*

combination of sound business acumen, innovation and craftsmanship, the success of Spode was assured.

Visitors to the Spode factory today can see pottery being created following the same methods and techniques which Josiah Spode perfected more than two centuries ago. The Spode tradition has always been one of innovation, however, and new techniques , particularly in the fields of quality control and firing, are continually explored and adopted when completely compatible with the Spode ethos. Just as Josiah Spode responded to the needs of his day, so Spode today remains closely in touch with

lains with the inclusion of bone ash. Evidence suggests that Josiah Spode was very close to perfecting his formula for bone china in 1796; he died the following year, but we know that his son, Josiah Spode II was successfully selling bone china by 1799.

It was Josiah Spode II who was responsible for marketing the company's products. In 1778 he opened a showroom and a shop to sell his father's wares in Cripplegate in 1778, and by 1784 he had appointed another Staffordshire man, William Copeland, as a travelling sales represen- tative. When Josiah Spode I perfected the process of blue underglaze printing in 1784, there was a ready market for these products because in that same year the tax on tea, which had previously been prohib- itive, had been dramatically reduced. This obviously led to an increase in the amount of tea which was drunk, which in turn led to an increase in the demand for teapots and tea services as more and more families became regular tea-drinkers. It seems probable that the Spodes had antici- pated the tax changes and its conse- quences, and prepared themselves to take advantage of the market. So, with the

customer needs. Every year new patterns, decorations and special items are created, but always with the authentic Spode touch. There is a commitment to maintaining individual skills, flair and talent, creating distinctive shapes and decorations, and pursuing excellence rather than settling for what is convenient to mass produce.

There are also collections of Fine Bone China and earthenwares on display to visitors, including

Top left: *The last Spode bottle oven, a feature which once dominated the Stoke-on-Trent landscape.* *Centre:* *Cutting out transfer prints from the transfer paper for each piece.*
Right: *A production worker removing ware from a kiln.*

The Blue Room which is devoted entirely to elegant displays of blue Spode, showing over 300 different items of the highest quality and beauty in a unique setting. Many of the designs will be familiar, and it is fascinating to discover just how far back their origins go - Blue Italian, for example, has been in continuous production since 1816 and is still popular today; the first version of the Willow pattern was produced about 1790.

How proud Josiah Spode would have felt, had he guessed that tableware produced in his factory would continue to bring pleasure to so many generations, and that over two centuries later craftsmen would still be making beautiful tableware in his factory, using the methods he developed.

Left: A collection of Spode's blue Imperialware from left to right, from the top shelf: Botanical and Floral, Girl at Well and Woodman, Willow and Rome. **Below:** The front gates to the Spode Works. The buildings date from the late 18th Century.

*The Trent &
Mersey Canal in a
picture dating from
1954*

ACKNOWLEDGMENTS

MRS LILY COPE

THE WARRILLOW COLLECTION, KEELE UNIVERSITY LIBRARY,
KEELE, STAFFORDSHIRE

PORT VALE FOOTBALL CLUB

THE POTTERIES MUSEUM

ALAN TAYLOR

IAN SHAW

THE WEDGWOOD MUSEUM